The Face of Creation

Also by Jascha Kessler

POETRY
Whatever Love Declares
After the Armies Have Passed
In Memory of the Future

FICTION

An Egyptian Bondage & Other Stories
Bearing Gifts
Death Comes for the Behaviorist
Classical Illusions
Transmigrations
To Kolonos

TRANSLATIONS
The Magician's Garden, 24 Stories by Geza Csáth
Bride of Acacias: Selected Poetry of Forugh Farrokhzad
Under Gemini: Selected Poems of Miklós Radnóti
Rose of Mother-of-Pearl: A Fairytale by Grozdana Olujic
Medusa: Selected Poems of Nicolai Kantchev
Lo! The Guiding Dawn: Selected Poetry of Táheréh

PROSE
Lee Mullican's Guardians
(Galerie Schreiner: Catalogue Essay)
Amalia's Chairs (Catalogue Essay)

# THE FACE OF
# CREATION

## CONTEMPORARY HUNGARIAN POETRY

### TRANSLATED BY JASCHA KESSLER

WITH MARIA KÖRÖSY, JULIA KADA, VAJDA MIKLÓS AND SARA LIPTAI

COFFEEHOUSE PRESS :: MINNEAPOLIS :: MCMLXXXVIII

Many of these poems, sometimes in slightly different versions, have appeared in the following places. They are: *The Hungarian Pen, The American Pen, Mundus Artium, The New Hungarian Quarterly, Confrontation, UT Review, Marilyn, Stand, The New Lugano Review, Arion, The Paris Review, The Massachusetts Review, The American Review, Contemporary Quarterly, New Letters, Red Weather, The Gramercy Review, Nimrod, Westways, The Spirit that Moves Us, The California Quarterly, Blue Buildings, The Michigan Quarterly Review, Midstream, The Literary Review, Cutbank, The Christian Science Monitor, The Kenyon Review, PN Review, Prism: International, Modern Poetry in Translation, Poetry/LA, Kenyon Review, Practices of the Wind, Poetry Now, Graham House Review, Ploughshares, The Missouri Review, The Virginia Quarterly Review, Art & Poetry Today (New Delhi), Visions, Rubicon, The Malahat Review, Hayden's Ferry Review.* For permission to publish and to reprint my translations, I am grateful to The Magyar PEN Club.

The publisher wishes to thank The Soros Foundation, and the Dayton Hudson Foundation for a grant from Dayton's and Target Stores.

Photograph of Jascha Kessler by Elizabeth Burr

Photographs of the authors and author biographies courtesy of Hungarian PEN.

Copyright © 1988 for this translation, by Jascha Kessler.

Coffee House Press books are available to bookstores through our primary distributor: Consortium Book Sales and Distribution, 213 East Fourth Street, Saint Paul, Minnesota 55101. Our books are also available through all major library distributors and jobbers, and through most small press distributors, including Bookpeople, Bookslinger, Inland, Pacific Pipeline, and Small Press Distribution. For personal orders, catalogs or other information, write to: Coffee House Press, Post Office Box 10870, Minneapolis, Minnesota 55458.

Library of Congress Cataloging-in-Publication Data
The Face of creation : contemporary Hungarian poetry / translated by
  Jascha Kessler.
        p.     cm.
    ISBN 0-918273-20-X (alk. paper) : $11.95
    1. Hungarian poetry—20th century—Translations into English.
    2. English poetry—Translations from Hungarian.     I. Kessler, Jascha
Frederick, 1929-
PH3441.E3F3 1988                                        87-34205
894'.51113'08—dc19                                     CIP

# CONTENTS

# TRANSLATOR'S PREFACE

On my first visit to Hungary, in 1972, I was accompanied everywhere by Julia Kada, a woman in her late 20's, who had been assigned to me by the Magyar Poets, Essayists, and Novelists, the Magyar PEN Club. She was then a recent graduate student in Anglo-American Literature. She is a first-rate English speaker and a lover of literature. I was full of innocent queries about Budapest, its architecture and history, and some of them may well have been embarrassing or even unfair. She often answered with a deprecatory giggle, "I've already told you: this is a comic operetta country from the early ice cream age!" Probably this young woman from a working class background was using that tag from some nightclub satirist to avoid any comparisons between her tiny nation of ten millions and what she thought an American poet stood for as the representative of a massive, serious and advanced efficiency — our nation of over two hundred fifty million . . . and a world language. Still, the Magyar poets are neither frivolous nor lightweights. And poetry was our task: every day for three hard hours during most of that month of July. Hungarian poetry is rooted in a complex social and political history reaching back about a thousand years. A history difficult for someone from the Western Hemisphere to grasp, and one that remains baffling and problematic for the Hungarians themselves.

What had taken me to Hungary? Chance. I had long hankered after the poems of Endre Ady and Attila József; but the language, not being Indo-European, is impenetrable, one feels, without prolonged study and residence in Hungary. And of course, there were "the events of 1956," as they are referred to today. The uprising had caused a certain amount of excitement among some poets here, and there were suddenly poets-in-exile among us. I had written my only sestina, "Budapest, 1956," in response to those fearful days of October and November 1956. (It appears in my first book of poems, *Whatever Love Declares*, and in translation into Hungarian, in *Gloria Victis*, a volume that gathered the poems written in many languages about the uprising.) I had also been sent a dozen or so poems by one of the emigré poets, and with the help of a student at UCLA, I had translated them in 1962-63. (They appeared in *From the Hungarian Revolution*, edited by David Ray, Cornell University Press, 1966.) Then, in September of 1971, I spoke at the 38th International PEN Congress in Dublin. At the end of that week, and after the banquet in the hall of the National Library, I found myself carried off to my friend Anthony Kerrigan's flat in Fitzwilliam Square, where a small group continued the party. Among those guests was László Kéry, head of the English Department at Budapest University. There was talk until the small hours. To resolve our questions, Kéry challenged us to visit

Budapest and see for ourselves whether or not poetry lives there in our time. Neither Kerrigan nor I knew how that should be made possible. Kéry was, however, unfazed: "I'll invite you myself!" he smiled. And lo! six months later an invitation for a month's stay in Hungary arrived in my mail. It turned out that that strong and good man, an expert in English literature, was also the General Secretary of the Magyar PEN, editor of its *Hungarian PEN Magazine*, and also of *Nagyvilag* ("Wide World"), a journal that translates fiction, poetry and criticism from many languages into Hungarian.

At that time I was unaware of the program that Kéry headed, one which invites American, English and Canadian poets as well as French and German writers to Hungary to work at bringing the Magyar poets to the attention of the world outside. The Hungarians are painfully conscious that their literature is hidden by the pecularity of their tongue. And, being enamored of their language and proud of the poetry that has been made over the last century and a half, they support a regular translation program. They have always been a very proud people; their situation in Central Europe has been labile for centuries; and their history is a tapestry shot through with error and tragedy: the results of which are that there seem to be as many Hungarians living dispersed through the world as there are within their borders. Their language and their poetry unites them, however; their difficulties and their many defeats have only served to make them the more proud, rendering their spirit complex and ironic.

I worked during that July of 1972 on several of the poets in this collection. I visited Budapest again in November of 1974 to read some of my own poems at the Magyar PEN, and took another batch of manuscripts back to Los Angeles with me. In July of 1977, I was invited for yet another month's work. Kéry and Miss Kada once again arranged meetings, Sunday visits in the countryside round about Budapest, dinners, parties, and so forth, so that I could meet other poets, hear their voices, and get a rudimentary sense of their conversation, their persons, their "styles." They were all most hospitable, and of course interested in having their work published in English. Most of them have some English, as well as French, German, or Italian, so it wasn't always necessary for Julia Kada to act as an interpreter, which she did superbly in any case.

I visited in April of 1979, and again in May, when I was pleasantly surprised. Invited for what I thought was a poetry-reading session at the PEN headquarters on Vörösmarty Square, I found a more than a dozen poets waiting — but they had come for my sake this time. I was presented with the Hungarian PEN Club Memorial Medal, the first American writer to be so honored, for my translations, which include two books: *The Magician's Garden: 24 Stories* by Geza Csath (d. 1919), published in 1980 by Columbia

University Press (republished in 1983 in paperback as Opium, by Viking Penguin), as well as *Under Gemini: The Selected Poems of Miklós Radnóti*, published in 1985 by Ohio University Press. I was a guest of the Magyar PEN yet again in December of 1983.

The Hungarian poets have long been a guild of great translators from many languages into Hungarian: small nations with high literacy, an achieved literature, and a large stake in European culture always take in a great deal more than Americans care to, for whom neither sophistication nor international currents of thought, nor for that matter a love of poetry, seem to matter, so far as the life of the mind is concerned. But (among educated people) in Budapest, ideas and their literary expression are the rule, not the exception. Because of the country's compactness, and its people's ear for music and language, everything gets turned into Magyar: poesis is a living property of their tongue. In short, there is still magic in the speaking of the language. There had even been discussion in 1972 over the use of the word "Metro" for the new subway line being dug: Metro is a foreign word. It was going to be allowed only because the first, short subway line built in Pest in the 1890s was called "Metro" after the one in Paris. The liveliness of the debate was only partly chauvinistic; unlike the French, they are not lexically dictated to by an Academy. Rather, it's a question of how to transform all things foreign into Magyar, as best suits their unique linguistic situation.

At any rate, in 1972 I began seriously working at translating. The work has gone on year by year, encouraged and aided by László Kéry and the Magyar PEN Club. My method is the same used by most of the other poets travelling to Budapest: collaborative translation. The challenge is to make poems in English. Obviously, the wise decision Kéry made stems from his recognition that poets ought to do this job, not people who don't write poetry professionally in their own language. My goal is to be accurate in conveying the content, that is, the meaning of my original, and also to be true to the form as well as the tone and rhythm of the thought. To say what the poet says, but in English. I have worked with two people intensely devoted to their Magyar poets, Julia Kada and Maria Körösy, and for a few poems with Sara Liptai also. I have also worked with that most knowledgeable and supersubtle editor, Miklós Vajda, the Literary Editor of the *New Hungarian Quarterly*, an English-language journal.

My method is simple: I ask for the original to be set down, and I ask for a word-by-word translation to be placed beneath, or beside it. And I mean precisely that — word-by-word in the original syntax, so that I can get a sense of the way things are said in Hungarian, without that veiling that begins with the mediation of a syntax rearranged to look English. Then, I query the connotations, symbols, metaphors and similes, their weight and force; etymology, antonyms, proverbs, slang, colloquialisms, down to the single noun, verb, adjective. It takes time: hours have passed over a phrase. Hungarian, being an agglutinative language, if that's the correct linguistic term, presents the English speaker with formidable structures, what becomes a whole stack of English words packed into one very long, strange, or obscure Magyar expression. Sometimes the "polyword" seems exotically primitive. Then I set about seeking a way to say it as we would say it in English, or rather American (for my translations, when compared with English and Canadian translations, are obviously American). I try to find our equivalents, parallels, associations, and so on. I freely admit that beyond my occasional recourse to a dictionary (the Hungarian-English one by László Országh), and my use of the thesaurus and an encyclopedia, I rely on the unconscious, or wherever inspiration comes from. Often, it evolves from my memory of the poet's speech. Sometimes there is serendipity; sometimes there is an ESP effect (or cause?) — it seems like what ESP would be were you "hearing" an alien, some envoy from beyond the Magellanic Clouds who is sending his thoughts into your mind, in English yet! One rule I try to observe: my lines repeat the poet's, my stanzas follow the poet's. When a poem is metered and rhymed, my rhyme scheme and meter try to follow suit. Rhyme-pattern is manageable; metric discrepancies will be inherent in the difference between Hungarian and English stress and cadence. Not as much as all that however, since Hungarian prosody is also quantitative. Were the original poems en face in this book the reader would recognize their similarity by their layout on the page.

Robert Frost said, Poetry is what gets lost in translation. That is so, as long as one thinks of poetry as the invisible, ineffable element of the poem's being, the way the "genius of the language" manifests itself to the native speaker. However, I assume that there are usually some equivalents in our different cultures, some similar developments in the self in the greater history of the Western culture. Hungary assures us of that: though it is Central European, it is a stubbornly westward-oriented nation. The world of the Hungarian Folk may be elsewhere, as it probably is for peasants in France. Hungarian, that is, is scarcely as alien as Japanese, Eskimo, Zulu, Urdu, or anywhere else outside Europe and the Western Hemisphere for that matter. Translation is not therefore impossible, or so it seems to me. What I hope is that both the qualities and the variety of my poets come through in my versions. I hope that even some measurable trace of "the poetry" may be found too. I have been told by Vajda and by István Vas that some of my Englished poems have turned out better poems: and when Vas wrote me this he was speaking of one of his own poems. If they say it, it may even be so. At least such generous criticism encourages me to imagine that I am offering not merely satisfactory but good things. If the reader feels that he or she has met these friends of mine from Hungary through these poems, then I shall be reasured. I only wish I could have done more of their work, for some of the writers here are copious and grand poets. And there are many whom I have not yet had the opportunity to bring into English. The good thing is that there are others also doing this work today: one hopes that the Magyar PEN may continue its effort, and that our acquaintance with Hungarian poetry will be augmented year by year. For sheer intelligence, wit, bravura and nobility, there are few contemporary equals. The Hungarians offer us an astonishing range of forms, great and imaginative lessons in metaphoric power, and above all, the vivid expression of fascinating personalities.

Jascha Kessler

Santa Monica, 1986

# WORDS READ IN A POEM
# IN A DREAM

It is by means

of poetry

that history passes

from the world

of the present

to the world

of the actual


Jascha Kessler

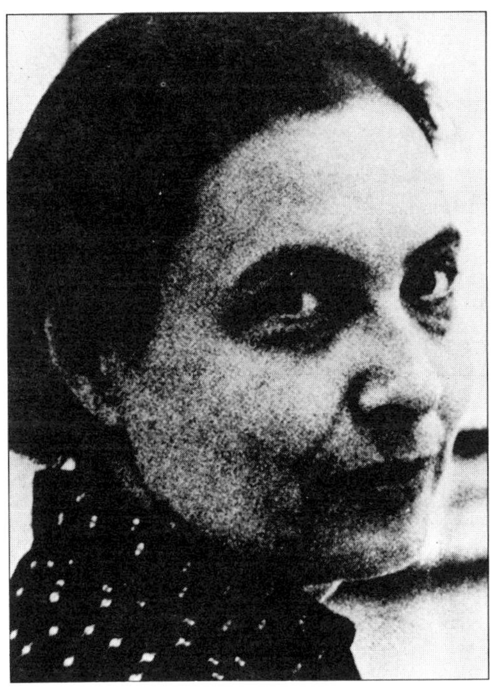

ZSUZSA BENEY: born in 1926 in Budapest to a family of intellectuals. She currently practises medicine as a lung specialist. Her books include: *Tűzfold / Land of Fire* (1972); Cérnahangra / For a Thin Voice (children's poems, 1972); *Rontás / Charming* (novel, 1974); and *A második szó / The Second Word* (1981). Writes literary essays and translates.

# A BROKEN GLASS

I. THE COLOR
Quite unimaginable, this blueness.
A dun-hazed dusk, a summer's ending, mild,
a sea dreamed from a shore dreamed by a child
might have been remembered with this blueness.

Arches far off ringing in dense, misted space;
a floe; black, wintry basalt, fogged-over,
creases veiling the frozen, sculptured face:
in the retina, secret blueness hovers.

Through the crack where space and time are shattered
the image falls amongst memories scattered
to be born again from the nuptials

of a scene and the dream-vision, lambent,
materializing in a different
being's dawning—poignant, unnameable.


II. THE BREAKING
It's almost stopped, just the way the bow stalls
for an instant at the top of the tune's
arch, which decays, collapsing in ruins
and silence at the edge of the air, and falls.

And hope's flashbulb is useless—having gotten
smashed to smithereens on the floor, and spread
the light that had pulsed in it on the dead,
glassy stuff like a clot, dried out and rotten.

That brief, imagined lightning stroke lies crushed
beneath its own dead weight, for it was slashed
by knowledge like the blade of a knife,

and beauty kindled by devastation
blazes from the heart of suffocation
like flames leaping high as they end their life.

III. REFLECTIONS
It's the boat plowing in its own furrow,
the waves gradually striking the shore,
though where it's gone one can't tell anymore—
into the past, or into tomorrow?

or it's like a falling star, perhaps,
that drags after it a droning wake,
its own memory striking stone in fire-flakes—
sobs erupt from the volcano's collapse,

and only when a whole shard makes its presence
known out of the heap of dead fragments
do words burst forth with memories together

to reconstruct what was sealed until then
into the world's mysterious glass, broken
again always, and always forever.

SÁNDOR CSOÓRI: born in 1930 in Zámoly, in western Hungary. Csoori studied at the now-defunct Lenin Institute (a language academy). In 1954 he edited a major collection of Hungarian folk ballads. His volumes of poetry include: *Felröppen a madár* / *The Bird Flies Up* (1954); *Ordogpille* / *Dragonfly* (1957); *Menekülés a maganybol* / *Escape from Loneliness* (1962); *Második születésem* / *My Second Birth* (1968); *Párbeszéd, sötétben* / *Dialogue, in the Dark* (1973). His collected poems appeared in 1975. He has also published a variety of titles in prose, including: *Tudósítás a toronybol* / *Report from the Tower* (1973); *Kubai napló* / *Cuban Diary* (1965); *Faltól falig* / *From Wall to Wall* (collected prose, 1969). *Nómad napló* / *A Nomad's Diary*, essays (Magvető, 1979); *Iszapeső* / *Raining Mud*, novel (Magvető, 1981); *Elmaradt lázálom,* / *Delirium Cancelled*, poems (Magvető, 1982); *A félig-bevalott élet* / *The Half-Examined Life*, essays (Magvető, 1982); *Kezemben zöld ág* / *A Green Branch in my Hand* (Magvető, 1985).

# THE SUNDAY BEFORE CHRISTMAS

Gold Sunday. . . . What shall I buy for you?
The sky's open, shops are open:
   a little more life, if I could,
      with the scent of pine-needles, because Christmas is coming.
Some sunny days out of the year
   and the big, unrelenting rain of winter
   to sweep me into the earth with you.
When you were still alive you made the chestnut's leaves
      kneel around my head,
      there was no death —
and oh what that ghastly change in place has done to me!
you're nowhere now and death's circling
    the dim rounds of the green jelly jars,
crawling out of my books
      like a starved ant on the tablecloth,
    darkness tagging along with it
    rage, shame
    an elbowing void approaching,
    your shroud and not your nightgown —
God, now I know why everyone goes mad who's touched
      by death, who tastes a chill strand of hair
    on the lips!
You make me talk to myself
      down Mártirok Street,
    the acid snow dripping from the eaves
    into my mouth drop by drop as on the condemned.


# E.K.'s WILL

Bury me in the overcoat if I die
it's very long, it covers my ankles
because even in the grass of summer I'm cold,
cold to the roots of my hair

# AFTERNOON OF GRAND OLD MEN

Lo, the afternoon of Grand Old Men!
Langourous, the lake shifts
and heaves like a rocker
and the cardinal points
of the compass suddenly land on the fence: four roosters.
Across the blueness the cock-a-doodle-doo of yellow
ruffling its plumage materializes.
Everything's stilled.
A wasp foraging
in a flower's fiery crater,
and stopples in the ears of the immortals.


# A STRANGER

Someone comes knocking, he wants lodging,
but like an android only capable of grinning at the doorknob,
at the rabbit ears' yellow flowers,
I mumble at him: Sorry, we've just had a death in the family,
we'd like to have a quiet wake,
talk to him beside the bread and wine,
the way our elders did,
and be together with the forest's sound he used to listen to.
He nods, standing there, a stranger in the midst of my mourning,
although he's Earthborn too.

# THE PRINT OF YOUR HAND

My mouth's full of snow,
full of snow again—
Who is there I could tell you've been dead for two hours?
I can tell only myself: the first stranger.
A scarf's round my neck, as though I was dressing
to go to you,
but I'm just standing under a crooked street light
on the forsaken hill,
the print of your hand on my scarf still.

# MAYBE ELEGIES

Maybe elegies have ruined me,
those slow, hovering, promiscuous birds,
because they taught me that I might live long, long
beneath a sky burdened with my name.

Which is why I've always loved big, lazy waters
that carried trees, suicidal butterflies, and that day from my life,
though I knew—ten more faces remained for the night,
ten deaths for the earth's next day.

After midnight's turned off the light
I can still reach the infinite,
and with my hand, as though I were touching
only a walnut leaf about to fly away,
the cold thigh of a woman who wants to wear a shroud
even on weekdays.

So I slip once more back to my body time
from the midst of timeless hours and timeless years
as blessed as someone bleeding to death in his dream
and smiling, his cheek half covered.

# REMEMBERING SNOW

Winter occasionally changes its mind
and starts in snowing,
heavy, desperate snow, as though fearful
of not making it stick through tomorrow.
The best thing then's disconnecting the phone, the doorbell,
boiling up wine on the stove,
riffling through old letters
and looking back on life as if it never
happened,
as if no cannon or lewd eye had ever glanced at me,
torn hands groped for my hand,
and whatever was politics, passion, bells ringing
were waiting for me again in some oceanic prospect—
rather, to dream
I could still lament my lost head,
that the wind's rushing through the lilacs
over beds, demi-bodies and rumpled pillows,
and that I'd be standing alongside the good ones
at the Earth's Last Judgment
in a polo shirt and sport coat,
beyond the smoke, barrooms, graveyards,
and staring a sublimely depraved country
in the eye,
the memory of snow in my head,
snow, snow silently falling
like the mortar of some cathedral.


# SUMMER, HALOED

A hornet flies into my room,
June's angel,
the curtain's yellowed by it;
the room's four walls,
forests, and wheatfields pass before

the sky's windowglass;
summer strolls in front of my mirror,
naked to the waist.
Around her head, the radiance of slick clay,
a halo of birds, and your face's halo
          that the June shower
has rinsed free of dust and death.
A tree outside, and a humming engine,
          the whistle of an otherworldly airplane—
oh, the big trips are over
just as you are somewhere, too,
only this is left: summer, hornet,
and gold streaming about me, cooling,
the dulled radiance of this world.


## YOU WERE STILL THE SUN'S THERE


I go north, up to the mountains,
to look at Matra's
russet woods again: the blue, yellow,
flame-red butterflies' campground
near the spring. You were still
intact there: a glowing masterpiece
beneath the leaves. Death's thunderous sting
fell into the abyss and not on you.
I go to look at that abyss,
the shadow of black flowers that rims it.
And I go on to that slow stream of stones
by Bearbone Rock. You were still
the sun's there: it shone through your skirt, through you,
through the haze of your pleasure and flesh; I go
higher, to the trees, to the mulberry's myriad eyes,
because I want to look at what looked at you,
and what of you is not buried yet.

ANDRAS FODOR: born in 1929 in Kaposmérő. He was a student at the Eötvös College, University of Budapest, and after graduation worked as a teacher in the Faculty of Arts. He also served as co-editor of the literary journal *Csillag,* or *Star.* Since 1959 he has worked in the Szechenyi Library, Budapest, concerned with library science and translation, and was awarded the Attila József Prize in 1956. His published work includes: *Hazafelé / On the Way Home* (1955); *Józan reggel / Sober Morning* (1958); *Tengerek, dombok / Seas, Hills* (1961); *Arcom útjai / Paths of my Face* (1967); *A csend szólítása / Addressing Silence* (selected poems, 1969); *Masik vegtelen / Another Infinity* (1970); and *Konyomat / Stone Print* (1982).

# FIELD HOSPITAL, 1945

The blast ripped off the railroad man's
right arm
and blew out both his eyes—
he wasn't depressed though,
only hoped it would all end,
and nothing worse happen to him. . . .
Blind, you can still tap telegrams out,
lefthanded.
                *

The doctor came down with the red typhus,
shrank to seventy-seven pounds.
His pregnant wife
heard from him, made it all the way from nowhere
by slow wagon
to see him.
Accosted the sentry
—showing her belly—
had to talk to her husband.
    A palm's raised with spread fingers—
five minutes!
    The man is lugged into the stuffy corridor
on a stretcher.
                        When they finally
get his bones up
on his collapsing legs,
the couple fall on each other's neck
like a pair of keys in a lock,
tongue-tied.

# YOUR BODY'S BREAD

Because you have shared the white bread
    of your body with me
doesn't mean you've been charitable
    or that I deserve it.

Call it predestination,
    fate's grace,
because we can't evade
    our ruination.

Because it didn't begin
    when I found you—
you opened your loneliness
    to me,

and it's not robbery, not selfish
    if I cling to you,
everything I am is smoldering
    in my skin.

As long as the woven willow of your fingers
    guards my neck like a basket,
even failing strength
    brings me nearer to you.

Though the day breaking hurts,
    night's a healing silence,
hold me hard while the doubled network of blood
    in our bodies flows, and never fear.

What good's believing in an afterlife,
    what can blind hope bring?
Riding each other's current,
    We need no other world.

GABÓR GÖRGEY: born in 1929 in Budapest. Görgey studied English and German at the University of Budapest, but took no degree. He has served as a staff writer for a national daily newspaper since 1959, and has published a considerable body of criticism, reviews, essays, and articles, in addition to four volumes of poems. His poetry titles included: *Füst és fény / Smoke and Light* (1956); *Délkör / Meridian* (1963); *Köszönöm, jól / I'm Fine, Thanks* (1970); *Légifolyosó / Aerial Corridor* (1977). Also a collection of verse translations into Hungarian from several languages. Author of many plays for stage and television, several of which have been performed in West Germany. Volumes of plays: *Komásszony, hol a stukker? / One Gun For Five?* (1969); *Alacsony az Ararat / Ararat is Low* (1971).

# ANATOMY OF A SUPPER

*He.* Can't exactly be named.
That is, can be called whatever,
any name hits the nail on its head,
he being there even in what's not he.
What's not he is in other words also he.
Everything, everyone
reducible in the end to this. *He*

*before.* Before what is as yet unknown.
Mere expectancy, as at a crucial
press conference,
reporters' and disciples'
lipwatching
to apprehend exactly before what this *before*

*willingly,* not picked up by force,
though this too he let come according
to ritual procedure. Millennial
convention of warrant for arrest. Stooges' hide and seek.
Ideotheology of corporate
interests. Sadistic orgy
of those in need of succor. But just because
he let it come, that is *voluntarily*

*turned in.* What? Exhibit A?
Enemy's letters
of commission? Espionage kit?
Reports in disappearing ink?
No doubt something had to have gone down
if he delivered it up. Though what? *Turned himself*

*in,* no code,
no hidden transmitter, no gun,
but all he had:
corpus mystidelecti. Right there, *himself*

*to torment,* though if there's anyone who
can set the stages of death by torture,
who might that be? Who, weeping, looks

hectically for logic
in the story's baffling chaos,
moreover, dispensing
useful advice
while his guts are shoved about.
Giving it all to *torment,*

*saintly,* put it like that, another name
for the unnameable.
Who, supping with premonitions,
at that measure in the treacherous
overture when
the unseen conductor raps for
tomorrow's anticipated nausea,
when the family physician's
going to declare: cancer! —even then the *saintly*

*and* venerable, like some
prophetic old man,
despite the foreshadowed teleological terror
flickering over his young man's face
every time he looks at
workable lumber,
mortised and tenoned,
full of potential splinters,
though he gets it together again—
*and venerable*

*took into such hands his own*
biopsy like a surgeon,
that smear torn from his own body,
slidemounted, indicating its
global metastasis, *took into such hands*

*some bread, bloodless flesh,*
*broke it,* and it seemed bones
crunched in it, sinews,
fiber, bread veins
tearing away in his gentle pressure
as he *broke it,*

*Gabór Görgey* / 15

*gave it to his disciples*, who, waiting
perplexed, would have preferred
falling to finally, famished,
only today somehow
it's all different, something's up,
he too's fussing
too much,
and what is more embarrassing
than your stomach rumbling
during solemn, softspoken words, and he really
*gave it to his disciples,*

*then said the blessing*, not giving thanks for
getting away with it again,
wriggling unscathed out
—unlike the others haha—of the cataclysm
with a joyful song, caressing his precious life
for the total-scanning, omnipotent
Giant Radar Screen,
not for that, but for the buffeting
on its way, *said the blessing*

*and spoke*, articulating precisely,
in words sans panic,
masking terror's sweaty fetor,
though the droning
of the desert shaman
was even then slowly ascending to the brain,
but he
drove it down in its pit, *and spoke, saying:*

*Take it*, while the taking's good,
don't pass up the chance,
don't wait, because tardy hands
will stir and cram the void
into the empty dish,
all chatting away like the crowd
at an embassy affair,
*therefore now take it*

*and eat,* some of this unsleeping kitchenmaids'
transubstantiated kneading
in a desperate dawn,
some of this bodily warmth
from a bakery glimmering away into the stratosphere,
take it easy *and eat*

*all of you,* that is each one of you,
hence everyone, which means no exceptions,
I mean all of you
who are and will be,
no conditions, or quota —
no, no, yes — *all of you*

*since this is my,* not that I actually know,
this is strictly speaking foreign matter,
still, mine own thing, so had to get used to it,
easy it wasn't, but finally I made it,
though naturally now that success arrives
I must part with it
(which is the way it goes,
that much I've caught onto here)
parting with it, *since this is my*

*body* (no more of this for now,
yes, I grew used to it, yet anyway
I have some doubts, far-out type,
take that time in the desert when he . . .
but let's let that drop, suffice it that:
you almost had me fooled there) *my body,*

*for you,* for you alone,
for endless links of your great-great-grandchildren's
grandchildren, since I've included
all future chromosomes
down the ages, theirs the food
*for you*

*given,* not because that's the way it is,
not apportioned and not trimmed to fit
the bed your soul makes and not like
dropping a donation in either, and you owe
nothing if you take some. . .
purely and simply this: *given.* (Silence.)

Gabór Görgey / 17

*After supper* the geological panorama
of shifting bowels, slaughterhouse
of razed villages and towns
laid over the peristalsis
reconstituting the world,
a wafer moon swimming
slow through the dark sky
*after supper*

*the same way* (same way exactly?
there was no foot to shove
the table further off
plates didn't slide
did the hand move from this place to this same place?
didn't the aerial corridor extending from the edge of the
    table
change from beginning to end?
and was it a hand unchanged?
what were those eons in the relative minute doing
during the metabolism of cells, toxins, sclerosis?)
let's say however: *the same way*

*he took it*
(ibid., cf. above, repetition)
*he took*

*a cup*, plain prototype
of any number of museum specimens, or, maybe
a wooden beaker
smelling like a cask soaking
wine up forever
and holding it till it rots apart
or is tossed on the fire,
the way the body holds its blood, moisture
and smell permeating it
(well, if we reduce it from
the goldsmith's triumph, we're merely
complicating matters) *a cup,*

*and again* these reiterations,
as though it's always the same,
even if nothing's ever the same,

but the spooky dreamlike déjà vu
goes on haunting,
because somewhere something sometime
as though over and over, and again

*said the blessing*, whatever he could
greened out of the desert interior

*and, yes*: and, world-conjunction,
the honeyed ands of similitudes,
the one-phrase lingo of kids
gabbling beatific ands,
this everything's—everything's semblance,
metagrammaticophysics
jargoning essence and chronicity: *and*

*said*, as he himself might have expected,
had he not spoken but been spoken to,
thirsty for some big
meaning—but now abandoned
in solitude's lunar vistas, *said:*

*Take*, that identical "take" once more,
but I've been around some since,
I've logged vast distances on my self-inflicted
sidereal stationary pilgrimage,
but anyhow again that *take*

*drink*, it'll be hard work
belting enough to wash this supper down,
I know it's the wrong moment,
something's squishing round like
an inky squid in your bellies
and needs to be flushed,
and it's not the broken loaf
but some older food in there,
I say, *drink,*

*all of you*, that is each one of you,
hence everyone, which means no exceptions,
I mean all of you
who are and will be,
no conditions, or quota—
no, no, yes—*all of you,*

because this is my, I'm forever confused
by the grounds of my proper dominion
because I could never actually be pervaded
by what's mind
and what is not,
in all the wealth of creation
happiness for me is a
perfect flaying,
which is just why I tell you, *because this is my*

*cup of blood*, could be it's also just one more find,
some mystical dimension turning up
for analysis in the universal lab,
though it's pretty much come down
right from the maternal side, a red and white
corpuscle-combination adapted to
Asia Minor's climatic/nutritional requirements
so here is this *cup of blood*

*which for you*—get it?—*for you*

*is poured*
the will-be-broken, the poured-out
are just words, but then
at that moment, alas, the body
shall reveal what a body is,
what power unbeatable
its frailty,
yet somehow I'll cope
when it's *poured out*

*sins*, whatever can those be, naturally it would be nice
    knowing,
every age frames
different offenses,
now this, now that, constituting deadly sin,
yesterday's deadly sins creditable today. However,
I could care less for brokers
on the morals market,
the law not counting for me,
my measure making blessed the sorrowing,
since my one concern's
universally tilted towards *forgiveness of*

*sins.* (Pause. Those who can,
drink.) *Then:*

*Do this*, no more,
moreover no matter what comes
of it, do only
*this*

*in memory of me.*
(I desire no more,
no tombstone, no pantheon.
On my grave unseen
a pebble's enough, a thought
of me by anyone.)


## INTERVIEW


I
I'm fine, thanks.
Teeth
in good shape.
Some hair, yes. I hope
it stays on, who knows.
Yes, family.
Naturally—why, don't I look
like a man who loves life?
It's brushed me, twice.
Vitality and style.
Size 12. Yes, a little large.
I've quit, finally.
I wouldn't know.
This and that.
Here and there.
Lots.
Have a smoke? Coffee?
Any other questions, Miss?

II
Visions? Haven't any.
Shoving on step by
step through some
inimical stubborn
jungly stuff as sly
and tricky as a rogue beast,
clawing it out of the ground
down to the bone
I make what I can of it.
In childhood, once upon a time,
I had visions, lots of them,
poetic, the real thing.
But it stopped, just like that,
when I started writing poems.
Visions. What I get's the old shaft.

III
Favorite dish?
If you could pour
some of that brisk-smelling
mushroom sauce over
the High Tatra and garnish it
with a crisp salad of Maytime
pastures awash in a dressing
of fat dew—I'd gladly dine on that.

IV
Well now when the rooftree
caved in on me,
we thought at first
it had to be woodworms,
then some unclassified
European species of termite—but
the fault was simple,
natural decay.
My headwound's healed,
finally.
More or less.

V
Our forefathers?
When they were building
Sumatra City
these tigers and antelopes
hopped into their heads.
There's supposed to be a Mongolian still alive,
a wonder-working shaman somewhere
who could purge them,
but they've never had time
to go for the cure
because of all their congresses
and official parades.
So the tigers have come down to us,
and the antelopes, their feed.
Still and all, that grand Sumatran
housingproject was neat;
it's a pity they couldnt get it finished
and the city of the future
was swallowed by the jungle's
green fire.
O good old days.
O heroes of yore.


VI
Maybe those monstrous
yoni-forms can never
be forgotten.
The herd clatters over
the feet of the tit-towers.
Worships milling
in the acorn groves.
Thighs in the iron grip
of ecstasy.
Tranced continuum.
But on the other isle
those who saw with refined fear
what was happening to love here
felt their manhood
shrivelling,
so scared not even Circe

could have stroked their fountain up.
That's it. We can choose between
boys grunting in rapture
or those with the withered balls.
Because it's hard, oh hard, hard
to be Odysseus clearing out
in his black ship, Miss.


VII
Snow? I like it, yes.
Sometimes though it seems
to sort of blend in
with the Sahara.
Discrimination's so difficult
these days, don't you think?


VIII
What I think of sleighs—
since you've asked me, Miss—
the sleigh's a useful vehicle
in winter.
And the bell
on the horse's neck is
perfectly ravishing.
But watch it there: when you coast down
from the shepherd's lofty, cheesey hut
to the cafe,
keep a fur hat and good sheepskin handy.
Because up there the frost's
tolling.


IX
That rock-artist howler?
Sure I know him! We chatted
for hours the other day.
He told me extraordinary
things about Early Medieval Russian
icon painting.

X

I'll tell you about that, too.
I was led
to a girl's boudoir
packed with masked bandits.
I had to rescue the virgin
who gratefully gave herself to me
in that pink and white decor.
When it was over we went
for a ride, a cloud of lace floating
fragrant on the horse's rump.
Finally we rowed, I think,
on a pointillist pond
So that's what happened
to me in the *Jeu de Paume*.


XI

They sawed some
left-over gaslights
in half.
The iron torsos
line the embankment
where lovers stroll.
They are kissing, and
from the black, cavernous stumps
the hovering, sweet, insidious stench
of gas surrounds them.


XII

The racket of that locust-colored
Diesel train running along
the other shore of the lake
can be heard even from here.
It's coming round the bay
one fine day
right to our house. O, Miss,
why won't you take it from me:
a man can't see those tracks coming
till they run through his room
right over my bed?


*Gabór Görgey* / 25

XIII

Like linens stacked
with love's fragrant lavender
in grandmother's cupboard—
in the terminal wards
old age homes
despair, loneliness
catarrhal laughter
vitamin deficiency, bedwettings,
fiftyseven varieties of cancer
lined up, neatly catalogued.
Isn't it adventurous of us
to lay our doddering folks
away so scrupulously in lavender?

XIV

These bugs live
only a couple of hours.
They've got it made, though.
Excavator-legs, prismatic lenses,
radar-sensors and a perpetual motion
sexual subsystem.
With supersonic wings extolling
nature's sophisticated engineering.
Naturally, because millions of years
of labor have been invested
in each
bug,
born in glory
just to drop dead in an hour or so.

XV

You see this little saw:
my tamed beastie.
When we go hunting
it perches on my fist,
and when I release it
prey falls from its path.
When we're tired out
we don't bother counting
the dry branches and twigs strewn about:
it goes to sleep on its nail,
my steel-taloned bird.

XVI
What I admire?
Concentration of soul
giving you the strength,
for example, to burn yourself alive.
And the iron calm
of the citizen in me
listening to the 8:00 A.M. news
and cracking the second
soft-boiled egg.
so essential to his existence.


XVII
It's a big fat hypothesis, of course.
But well-constructed, even
a Martian could see that.
I admit there are other
palatable hypotheses, but
I'm not about to kowtow
grovelling in the dust
with the rest of them
every time the tribe's adored totem-face
stares at me.
My backbone's no thrilling conductor
of cultural currents —
in fact I'm turned off:
because these days it's not just
connoisseurs of the primitive
but conquerors too who
ooze goodwill.


XVIII
You can't mean that.
Absolutely ridiculous.
I don't believe my ears.
Maybe I got it wrong.
You wouldn't mind repeating what you said?
So I heard you right! I'm
just appalled, Miss.

XIX
Were you there, too? You got to see
that fabulous well, didn't you,
where tourists take the plunge
from the edge, immersing themselves,
doing the antique abyss?
A marble phallus
broke off under me and I lost
interest in the whole trip,
but take my word for it
I was the only tourist
with that kind of luck,
and I brought home an empty soul.
That indefatigable American woman though,
what a thirst for culture she had, and
what a splash she made, ye gods!

XX
Those pencils you're taking notes with
are the best there are.
Carried only by that hole-in-the-wall place
between Scylla and Charybdis.
You reach the overhanging cliff
by water, in a skiff,
and the sea's monster fins thrash
so madly here
even the saltiest pirates
won't go out unless
you come up with a
really heavy tip.
But if you do make it
in a weathered skiff
and get out alive—
you'll find the best pencils
on earth
there.

XXI
All this, to go it alone,
for its own sake, and mine?
For what,
to perfect myself?

Polish it off
like an honor student
with a 4-point average?
Show
what great time I ran,
the champ, me?
To pick up a cum laude metaphysical
degree later on?
So as to jeer triumphant
at the rest
who couldn't swing it?
Even though the job
demands
personal dedication
you can't get your kicks out of it
unless we're in it together.
Only a stone lives alone.


XXII
Nice to hear that, Miss.
I do make a point
of shaving close, yes.
It brings in this sort
of mini-success, among others.
But after razoring it clean,
deep-rubbing my wincing face —
how the lotion bites —
behind its contented grin

a bit of that endless rope of pearls
stringing out through the earth
exposes itself:
the Homo Sapiens mandible.


XXIII
Yes, memory's the problem.
What I don't recall, just
isn't. Life after death
will only be perfect
(I mean, refined from earthly dross)
if they can sublimate my
dematerialized matter

out of all recollection.
If, however, from the ranks of tremulant souls
I can't pick my mother out—
because memory's gone—
let me ask you, Miss, where's the point in it?

XXIV
Happiness?
Listen, all it takes
with this grace-contraption
is losing that one single
screw
and my ramshackle residence
of lights and shadows
tumbles down.
Happiness, it seems, is merely
a malfunction in the rhythm
of horror.

XXV
There it is.
Of course it is.
If it weren't, it couldn't be.
But since it is,
it must must be,
and if it must
it certainly is.


# SOME NOTES ON THE WIND

"Sound, majestic wind!" From an old notebook.
Might just come in handy. Never did though.
Sure, say anything.
But royal, no. So that's a lie.

Because even the way it comes.
The skulking wind.
(Royal! Makes me laugh!)
But foliage rustles.
Tippytoes,

Little rococco zephyr.
And they, lounging in the garden,
all together, immediately, just like that:
"Ah, Nature! Ah, soughing sighs!
Ah, pattycaking leaves!
Ah, that immanent music!"
Someone even says it: Zephyr!

Private lyric. Blooming. Old women.
And the sprite-fingered pest
(I refer to the wind)
throws a tantrum on the garden.
Which is why it hasn't. And sat in the notebook.

*

Shelley of course. Fascinated by it.
And yet he too.
From those windswept heights to some room.
Unwinds himself from his soaking cloak.
Door and window carefully to.
And then. Ode.

Or all those blustering cheeks!
Antique cartography,
And Aeolus, they blabbered, Aeolus.
And the lyre. And harp. That sort of stuff.
I can see it still, the old notice:
"Organ grinding on these premises prohibited."
Why just that?
Because, so much for your mythical hand organ too.
As far as I'm concerned.

Personification. Well, yes.
Good at it, those ancients.
We could use some of it too. And how!
Boiling up in this vacated pleroma.
Bulls, cheeks, heavenly rumps.
Quasi-immortals and their caprices.
Sexual metaphysics.
The caprice alone is left. And they nowhere.
Drafted right in the uterus.
No sooner discharged than summonsed
under penalty of.

*Gabór Görgey* / 31

And so back to earth.
Caprice. Caprice.

Like the wind.
Now it comes, now goes, now it blows, now rips away.
That's its broken-down atavism.
*
Say it pounces.
To scoop up the sea.
(As though it weren't just fine as is!)
Or millions of pollen-drenched
paratroopers.
At me. Because, that's all I need!

Panting forest of bronchi.
Coral reefs of mucosae.
Volcanic ranges of inflammation.
Lung sacs heaving like fish
on the ocean of suffocation
in the allergic dusk.
A landscape to him! How he enjoys it!
*
Just to give you that Vörösmarty touch. Tornado
says it for him in The South Seas Isle:
"The dust of the earth I eat,
I drink from the towering sea."[1]
Adding moreover (the poet):
"Whirled the waters and their floating fishes
into the clouds aloft."
Nor is that the best of notions either.

Poets, time to spit it out.
Cost what it may.
Global leper!
My putrid Job-boil!
You cruddy cataclysm!
I'll say even more: You besotted militarist!
Filth! Abortion! Abomination! Carrion!
Utter nobody! (That's the word, precisely!)
So, wind.
*

And I on this head in that old notebook.
     "Sound, majestic wind!"

No wonder such lyricism gags you.
Much more authentic if the lyrist.
Like Shelley. Sea, skiff, wind:
in this most poetic predicament
he couldn't swim but floundered off
without coming to loathe that exquisitely
melded . . .

Self-hatred alone
kills. Not death.
                *
Nothing more hateful
than ourselves.
O Spirited Lyrist!
With your souvenirs, your visions?
What are they worth these days?
Pouring it eternally
from grecian urn
to grecian urn?

Life dashes past.
                *
Face it? Speak up? Level with it?
Moral hangups, moral hangups,
gossip all over town about.

When all he had to do was just say it.

Or at least like Henry Heine (in "Homecoming"),
laughed right back in its face.
"The wind pulls its pants on,
watery white pants!"
(Fine metaphor for the royal wind:
grandma's flannelette undies) — now

dictators raging and old women
over his unpardonable grave.
                *

If once upon a time we said King—and it's no king—
we must say that once upon a time
we did say King—though it was no king!
Merely a racket devouring the silence.
Currency quotations changing
before the grave, after the grave.
Sublime stockbrokers lifting a finger
                    (raising the Host?)

although someone in the outer court is even now
gently swishing his scourge.
                    *
What more do I need? An adage.
Wait, wait. It's coming. Here we are:
"Better than memorial the memory,"[2]
(To quote yours truly.)

Memory, Memory? Sure! It's something!
If but a faint trace, still, that.
Of ourselves—in another. In a fisherman
(sometimes a human being's netted).
Something of us, light, floating, bright,
living in him:
"To the sea they used to go,
to pick periwinkles."[3]

That's nice. What Vörösmarty liked
(in The South Seas Isle).

[1]"The Southseas Isle," an epic poem by the 19th century Romantic, Mihály
Vörösmarty.
[2]The line is from one of the most widely-known poems of Sándor Petőfi,
"Late September."
[3]Again, from The Southseas Isle.

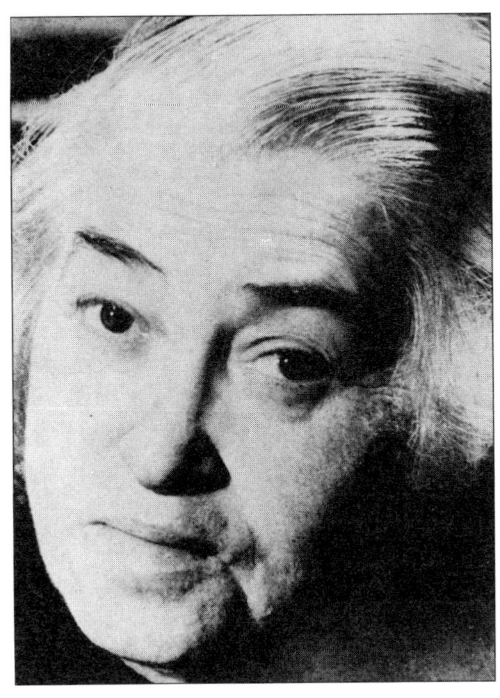

Anna Hajnal: 1907-1977. Hajnal was born in Gyepüfüzes, in Western Hungary. She studied English at a language academy in Vienna. She published thirteen volumes of poetry, including *Elhiszed nekem? / Do You Believe Me?* in 1976, and a posthumous collection, *Alkonyfeny / Evening Light* (1978).

# IMAGES

CAST ROSE
Withering under its bush,
poor thing, poor fading corpse
fallen into forever,
the bright garden of Hades,
whose boatman Charon's wind
has a million oars —
when he passes, a fanfare!
the garden, thrumming,
follows him
with a million sighs

DEAD GIRL
Soft she was, young
moon in the water
moon floating beneath waters
a form dreamt, desired —
she was — and gone, burning in water,
dreamed there, in the mirror —
the wandering one, sinking, rising
a moon drifting, light, alive

YELLOW
Running yellow time
the sun's carriage and moon's
whirling you
    over
        hill and dale
        you want to scream —
        it's running away —
        the yellow horse
            death

# I'VE NEVER COME AWAY, YOU KNOW

I
Walking on a child's tender feet
long ago, so long ago,
in the talking brook
the laving, brisk flow
could I ever have renounced it?

I've never really come away, you know,
I sit there still, the pebbles rolling
in the summer stream around my rock,
a waif weeping, torn with homesickness,
beaten away to this foreign world . . .

As for you on your side,
if my reply is laggard
while silence waits a word from me,
it persuades my duplicity too —
for in silence I joined my twin to me
expressing myself as I am now,
the one you see, and that child far-off — myself.

II
I can blush with shame, you know,
my brow burning with suffering,
fire in the clouded sunset —
where I lie in my twilight,

my heart a blade wiped clean
on the meadow's plush,
washed by the delicate grass,
hardened by faith,
may I be a sword, simplicity itself.

# MAY IT NOT RUN DOWN

Don't be fed up by it all, please! Keep turning!
so many of us carried along, the quick and dead.
O, how much longer? and I to ride on, insentient,
mere bones it offers to the sun,
casually! what other choice has it?
But I'm coming to think I know
what bathing in the gold pouring from the sun
is worth, or retreating into a soft corner
if winter returns: live! live!
we're scared, actually, all of us really scared
and hiding! all of us! tucked away
in hibernation, in the shadows, in the tall grasses,
in our caves! or homes, even air raid shelters
hiding from bombs and bullets underground,
and from teeth too! Please, don't notice us!
I hope I'm never number one in anything!
Imitation. Every leopard knows how,
and the tiger, the snake. Huh, what am I saying?
every lizard, the quail and partridge.
As long as I'm not a bird of paradise,
drunk on nectar, or marching under orders.
Oh, God, don't make me a killer, and don't get me killed!
because stopping, dying's my horror
Ah youth: I didn't know enough to be scared,
ending was at the end, how should I have known?
I, die? hardly . . .
but if it's true?
over the horizon, silence?

# RAINS

I
Is the flood growing to whelm us?
how dense the rain, pouring, booming
each morning pierced by the silvery lances
of thrushes braving its reckless chant.

II
Jet black trees stand like posts
in the black mirror
cranes cronk-crunkling, wild geese
whirring through the lacquered sky,

I'm made to be happy!
leaves falling, falling golden,
underfoot the lacquered sky
blooms freckled with gold—

III
Cousin Noah of old, till I die,
Noah hurdling towering waves
in my grand ark, preserving
the soul's happy creatures.

IV
She hides, timid dryad,
green, scalyfaced girl,
her green brows windcombed,
watching me through green tresses,
greenleaved tresses.
She sits in the trees, she swings,
silent in the wan moon, unsmiling.
She may be sad, my God—
how the wind booms, dark, lamenting,
all scales, she weeps, a green girl,
and from my heart
a virid-faced baboon
bawls in answer.

V

The green stream carried her off,
whispering, greedy, he swept her away,
hid her in a cavern's pool
where he handled her, hugged her,
dressed her in saltblue crystals,
an elfin statue
for his glassblue room,
his subterranean pool
where blind, tiny fish
surround her —

VI

What's my word? Love!
an apple ripening, meat, juice,
under its skin the future's tense
as the seed darkens!

What enfolds me? this moment!
life's greatness not mine to hold
I'm too small to take it in,
I wrap myself in my own caul.


## TREE TO FLUTE


You, my branch, my lopped limb! —
don't you cry, it's over, for you —
you were cut away, you've recovered —
for us it's being honed, the waiting axe,
and if it falls on us,
will we become a flute, desire weeping,
a sobbing, a quavering violin?
or lie silently, merely mute, lying?
the struggle's finished for you,
lucky flute: what more could you wish?

# THAT'S ALL?

Shearing, as the gardener
snips the sucker,
controlling wild growth
with shaping hands,
looking and choosing —
which bud's to be the branch —
rooting out, cutting or pardoning
by design and scheme:
trimming pyramids, tall arches,
scissoring bowers for gods —
how I'd love doing that —
taking hold of the passionate growth
in my unmastered heart.
Slicing through wild, winding
trailers, charming
with a bright, sharp blade —
to but loosen its hold on me!

release its hold?
and must the clasper wither?
trailers, leaves, tendrils droop?
A French park, my loving?
moderation, cautious suffering?
precise forms, narrow blossoms,
the reign of geometry,
is my calmness to be a tight calmness?

GYULA ILLYÉS: 1902-1983. Illyés was born in Rácegrespuszta, Western Hungary, son of a machine operator on an estate. He served in the army of the Hungarian Republic of the Councils in 1919, and fled the country subsequently, living in Paris from 1921-1926. His first volume of poems appeared in 1928. He is best known for *A pustak népe / People of the Puszta* (1934), which is partly autobiographical, combining sociology and literature; he added a sequel in 1962, *Ebéd a kastélyban / Luncheon at the Mansion*, which covered the changed conditions on the puszta of his childhood. He edited *Nyugat* and its successor *Magyar Csillag*, the most important literary magazine before World War II. Other works include: collected poems in two volumes, 1920-1945 and 1946-1968 (1972, 1973); new poems, *Minden lehet / Anything's Possible* (1971); a selected volume of poems in English (Chatto and Windus, 1971); *People of the Puszta* in English (Corvina Press, 1967); and *Petőfi*, a biography of the 19th Century poet, in English (Corvina Press, 1973). He has also published *Kháron ladikján / In Charon's Barge*, a prose volume of notes on aging. His last volume of poems was *Közügy / Public Concern* (1981).

# AFTERWARD

Of course, there'll be whimpers afterward,
    like the cur that licks
his master's shoes, and cringes towards
    the furious stick.

Afterward, and just because the smile of grace
    doesn't fall this way either, I'll attempt
to lean back proud as a lordly ruler, my face
    frozen with contempt.


# CANNIBAL FUTURE

They're collapsing, the ancestors
    who stood behind you.
Crumbling, done for,
    the wall you'd put your back to.

Alone — a grownup — here you stand.
    The tide's booming louder,
breakers swamping the land,
    the heartless, cannibal future.

Not behind — but there before you, there —
    an empty, howling waste.
A chicken squawking, a stampeding mare.
    You stand. Till something else turns up at last.

# IN DANTE'S WHIRLWIND

It droops towards death; yet look, sooner or later the leaf
throws itself down without prompting —
but when is its time? I saw it all. Sooner or later
all are hurled by the wind together into the mud.
We take each other's bearings. I you. You me,
        cohorts herded together —
and thus melded, mates in doom,
all in the very same trouble in all directions up against such things!
spinning, fallen leaves — like a fight, mates, a contest —
because finally it does count, who flies together on the
wings of our era, even if it's in a whirlwind out of Dante!

Vainglory carries us along. Vainglory is what struggles.
And because each moment promises eternal joy, the goal must be eternal too.


# ON AN INFANT

His friend the light is already cutting
        diamonds of intellect into his eyes.
He blinks. What does he suspect?
        What news does he bring?

# MY OLD MAN'S DAWDLING

The only one who'd appreciate my daybreak's
sudden sprint of spirit in this
grave-ready dawdling of mine
        would be the very one
who'd once dashed out, out, out —
        wakened by the first sunbeam —
out of winter's room, carried on child's legs, shoeless,
        or even naked,
        his face to the sky —
        into the year,
        into the infinite future,
        until now, now. . .he was taking off!




First published in Hungarian in September 1983,
after the poet's death.

MÁRTON KALÁSZ: born 1934 in Somberek, and grew up on a farm. Kalasz went to school in Pecs, in Southwestern Hungary. He has worked in cooperatives, was head of cultural centers, and served as a reporter to the Hungarian Radio and as a reader for Europa, a publishing house. He has also been a lecturer in Hungarian at Humboldt University in Berlin. On the staff of *Uj Iras / New Writing*. He has published eight volumes of poetry, including: *Hajnali szekerek / Early Morning Carts* (1955); *Ünnep elott / Before the Feast* (1961); *Éjféli körmenet / Midnight Procession* (1970); *Hírek Árgyélus / News for Argylenak* (1975); *Megszámított vigasz / Calculated Sympathy* (1976); and *Az Imádkozó Saska / Praying Mantis* (1980).

# GHOST PSALMS

*On the death of Johannes Bobrowski*

I

Neither the little Jewshops nor the complex wooden churches
      blazed on that day,
        nor was autumn's blue icon yet scarred.
He sat with his brandy, Johannes did, at his lovely porcelain lamp,
      musing over Tilsit's treelined narrow streets,
        and the fine lines of antique cars.

II

A long time ago, all that. Actually,
      he was on view in the town's murderous cockpit of a market.
        Barbarians, stallkeepers, fishwives ringed him round —
Here, they'd be muttering, sits a fattish man, a scribe maybe,
      in this jaundiced light. The plague-death alone knows
        what sins that man's assumed for himself.

III

And he ran, soaking foamed, the vengeful legionaries
      tumbling after. What's a village of hostages
        but a burnt flag. Groves of innards becoming gun-nests.
He was strong enough to believe himself a weapon amongst them yet —
      he is seen crossing on ferries, pontoons, beyond
        the sandy banks before the trees haze, blued . . .


# HYMN

    Where should I seat you, where
should I place the vase with its shaggy bouquet,
where should I set my favorite books out for you to notice,
what say to you or hand you when you ring,
and will that once-over on the pictures do it,
won't my daughter's little hands
      show up by lamplight,
how to lead round to this splendid carving,

that Roman fragment, these remarkable pebbles,
     my past, my children, my mother,
and that sometimes I madly think
     I've actually invented my own private theory,
though everything you see, chair, rug, mug,
stands hidden here in this mean cave, like me,
how suggest my loneliness to you,
     my loves, my misery,
          how reveal it all,
even my naked sobriety, when you're here at last,
     darling future?


## IMPROMPTU


Like Chopin, not even showing my puss,
letting my loved ones fume through the flat,
letting them hate me in the meadow, where
their outraged cries are braided in the poplars
like ribbons in hair — staying indoors,
writing, discovering short poems,
obstinately poems, neither French
nor Polish: both at last discernible
in them, and then in each other —
where's my country? where my poems
are so well made I count myself at home
in their nutshell; in their images the landscape:
poplars shining through, cries for crowns —
so I needn't even trouble stepping out for them.

# LEGACY

I don't see my mother dancing —
in my thoughts she still trims vines
sprayed blue with copper sulfate
for her two bags of wheat, eight bushels rye.
I don't know if her young face
was lovely, if the other tenants
admired her dragonfly form,
or if my blond father tethered his horse only
at our cabin in the wild Whitsun ride.
I just see her in the wintry dawn
chopping cornstalks at the stove
or patching sacks in the stilled yard;
I see her at evening in the vineyard
secretly taking flowers for my dead father.
Such memories pour into me,
and whirl me round fiercely now —
my mother, whom none could help,
in the darkness of whose flesh
the cancer spread its deadly arms,
who left her son this legacy.
This is not to blame her; not one curse
ever left her lips, I know . . . Only, poverty

took it all from her vein-roped hands.
Half a day she walked to find me, a hand
at some far-off farm, bringing me potatoes she spared,
spending her scant savings on my studies;
and when I scanned my first lines
at the window something silvery
glowed in her eyes — joy.
And then she was gone, never to see
the first book. I could thrust no money
secretly beneath her bolster, for a dress, for salt —
her bones in the graveyard
moldered to fat silent clay; now flowers force their roots
in summer where her forehead used to be.
And I carry her legacy for good:
on my face the mark of sorrow,

in myself humility's soundless load;
until I die I shall not forget
that world of grinding poverty —
in the field we are walking
like yoked horses together forever.


## MAIDEN


May that lovely young body of yours
leave but its bare trace of you in me!
My admiration's a straggling soldier's,
with just the sense his might be,

but I shan't seize you, shan't bite or eat
— that flesh of yours all so careless
and grown ripe though still so child-sweet,
where I have never been, even less

hope to come, no, how could I get there
or do anything . . . and all because
I've never felt my own years like this,
stunned by this moment that gives me pause —

it's hardly old age, no, the chaos
of my mere twentysix years
out of which one makes one's own shape,
too soon yielding like this to one's fears

even before one must; and just see me
putting on the cheery expression,
not the lean and hungry face when
conversation turns on passion . . .

Well, what you got from me was this:
a crock of crummy advice, plus
a little yearning self-pity, when
he's the one to redeem me thus,

yes he, even he should live now
for these coming few years in me,
making it worthwhile for him to step out
towards you like a soldier, free.

The nostalgia's as far as I go,
never reaching the words — you see,
the one looking at you's not this young
twenty-six-year-old, but only me,

older, tireder, the man virile
enough to note his tension, the wild,
secret explosion in his body
as he contemplates you, child;

but finds he lacks what it takes
to cast his avid net over you,
and hasn't learned the heroism yet
to feel his shame through and through.

Márton Kalász / 51

# NEARLY NAMELESS

for Zoltán Zelk

The dreaming animal cries out,
remembers its tears in the morning —

our own tears float vaguely up from memory's
profoundest strata,
a recollection resurrected merely as a poem,
a great dawning sun,
and so remote from the source;
no bird may drink at it,
nor any of our companions: only
a murmuring audible from the depth,
so nameless to the ear
it's nearly nameless to the soul —
not even an intimation of tears
in the poem as it's born.


# THE AGE OF SNOW

. . . what we've decided to call snow. — Gunter Kunert

I

    And the Age of Snow came. The ravaging migration came.
Came swooping down against the vacant fields. Stormed through
the reeling gardens to the churches. Whistled through the
pillared cities. Paralyzed airports. Occupied important buildings.
People stared from the windows. In factories a myriad movements
instantly froze. The air was carved by blue profiles. What had
happened no one knew. No one knew what lay in store for him.
    All this at the eleventh hour. When bells could have
been rung. The rush handled. Cafes dressed in white in time.
Reading rooms opened. The eighth bridge inaugurated. Busdrivers
changed. The cop on the beat. Movie programs.
    Workers feared going out the gates. At the gates they
feared searching them. People feared yielding their seats to

them. They feared having to sit.

     The invisible ones stared in each other's faces then. Not one
of them could be stopped. Not one saved.

     Rubbertreaded halftracks rolled patrolling. Everywhere,
neat little modern forts. Everyone walked between cyclone fencing.
Loudspeakers warned, Stay calm! Spotlights sliced the air. For
control's sake. Because darkness was growing.


II

Many noticed nothing, but nothing.
Believing dogma's stringent rules,
they shoved at the cause delivered them:
made folks offer up their coalstoves,
strip their rooms for the Big One's sake
and register their extra coats . . .
Now and then, halting their pushcarts
on the snowpack so drear, so cold,
they beamed beatifically
at the icy iridescence
of colored caps and scarves, dazzled,
and wondering what good they did —
what good to people, or themselves.

       "Oh, how strong are wintry lands,
       Bringing good to human hands."

Passersby never turned and stared:
long out of date, that sort of thing.
Everyone everywhere always
hearing pigeons coo at their backs,
dodging into espresso bars
to get some skin, dig the new tunes,
or sitting through those second acts
afraid to miss some hidden cue.
And at those dreaded rallies, yes
masked by three-day growths of stubble —
and masked by their own faces, too.

Márton Kalász / 53

# TIME'S NO GRAMMAR

Time's no grammar
rain weeps and falls to make me speak language
to it; May wind
blows through my skull, driving words ahead —
for my heart; the moment limps
spastically
until the sun comes out, and there! your grinding teeth
on the other side flashing some appeal —
watch it! murmur the delicate,
little banners of stucco tumbling in slow motion
back onto the walls now: from behind
they sift down on me from everywhere —
autumn's here, silent scraps of paper
mixing with the loud flakes of first snow.


# UP AGAINST THAT WALL EVERYWHERE

Up against that wall everywhere —
listening to invisible time
in the dark; then, at the core of memory
they set an earth-eating tot
in a dazzling garden; abandon it there —
knowing that I could sit here forever
moved by myself alone, nearly unconscious;
and whatever became of the good instinct, and trust —
that earth-eating tot's tiny palms flitting
so simply from creature to creature; has my consciousness
thus vanquished concept after concept —
the lips shaping, the trance casting words there;
the child seated, unerringly tucking away
the most mixed-up stuff of existence.

LÁSZLO KÁLNOKY: born in 1912 in the Northeastern city of Eger. After studying law in Eger, Pecs, and Budapest, he worked as a minor government official and librarian before World War II. Following the war he became a publisher's editor before devoting himself to writing and translating in the late 1950s. He has published three volumes of poems and an anthology entitled *Torn Masks* (1972). His most recent volume of poems was *Bálnák a parton / Beached Whales* (1983). His vast output as a translator includes Goethe's Faust Part II, Racine, Marlowe, and several volumes of lyrical poems from American, English, French, German, Italian, Russian and other poets, classical and modern.

# THE QUARRY

An apparently insignificant
young woman's trailing
me. She stops to scratch a note —
openly! But why?
Her very eyes say she knows all there is to know about me.
She's the water in the brook that vanishes
as I kneel by it, parched.
She's the rug unseen hands yank from under me
when I step on it, so I'll break my neck
on the marble floor.
She's the solid-seeming stair
though my raised foot
never finds it.
She's the three-minute egg
a shrieking bird flies out of
when I crack the shell. She it is who takes
a myriad shapes, a black panther
behind the secret door,
the velvet drape, though my hand
has not yet dared to lift it.
It seems she's insignificance incarnate,
the phial of poison
disguised as an innocent drink,
so tempting to a thirsty man
that sooner or later, when the heat wave's here,
I'll raise it to my lips.

# THE GLASS HAT

Back in the Twenties, Filippo Marinetti, Italian Futurist
    (later, Fascist)
poet, thought of making the glass hat modish. To get things rolling,
he had one blown at the Murano glass factory, and wore it around.
I couldn't pin down why this innovative hat
never became voguish, though I traced it back through Italian
LitHist, the glass industry's Trade Journals, and the men's hat
pages of the fashion magazines. I never managed to learn
whether Filippo Marinetti intended poets to distinguish themselves
from ordinary mortals, or else hoped the glass hat
would come into general use. If he'd succeeded,
more than one aging poet's chest might be puffed up with pride today
when a young writer tips his glass hat to him
on the avenue, or in the corridor of some publisher's office.
Though considering how brittle glass is, my heart hurts
when I read in the newspaper that one of my acquaintances
has unluckily lost an ear because the blow aimed at his skull
smashed the brim of his headgear. Of course, shatterproof glass
was also invented later on, though Filippo Marinetti
might not have accepted a chapeau made of it as
an authentic glass hat. Still, certain advantages
would have accrued, had his notion caught on.
For instance, if we should come across a clear fountain in the Dog Days,
we could simply hold out our hat under its flow,
thereby soothing our torturing thirst. After symposiums
of writers-and-readers in hick towns or on godforsaken farms,
we shouldn't have to stagger to the outhouse in pyjamas through
the subzero frost. We could make do by setting our hat under the bed
bottom up, as a pisspot. In the morning, of course, we should
remember to rinse the glass hat thoroughly before putting it on,
if we have some self-respect. There'd be nothing then to stop us
next year in the Dog Days, should we come across a clear fountain,
from holding it under its flow once more, and thereby
soothing the thirst that tortures us.

László Kálnoky / 57

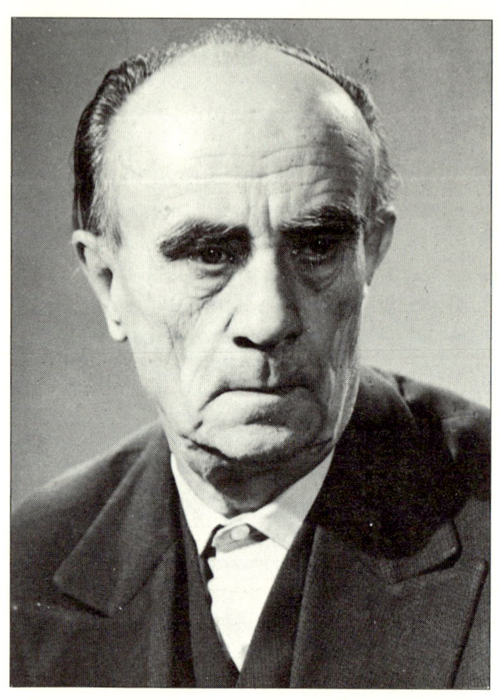

LAJOS KASSÁK: 1887-1967. Kassák was born Érsekújvar, which is now part of Czechslovakia, in a poor working class family. In his youth, he walked through Austria, Germany, Belgium, and Paris. Walt Whitman was an early formative influence on his work. A poet, novelist, short story writer, editor of journals, painter and organizer of exhibitions, Kassák was a leader of the Hungarian avant garde. Kassák was the author of many novels, an autobiography, *Egy émber elete / A Man's Life*, collections of short stories, books on art and painting, and many volumes of poems, with a collected volume in 1970. After a 1960 Paris exhibition, a great number of his constructivist paintings went into private and public collections in France and elsewhere. Kassák's poems are usually referred to as "untitled," or "numbered" poems. "#12" comes from *Máglyák énekelnek / Singing Bonfires* (1920); "42," and "#65" come from *Tisztasag konyve / The Book of Purity* (1926); "#96" from *35 vers / 35 Poems* (1931).

#12

my guts worn out by debts
I enlisted like a hick with fingernails still made of marmalade and eyes
popping out on the street corner at night leaning against the rainbow
I want
"TODAYNIKS"          "to be far-out trippers"
                     "RED PILOTS"
                     "VIRGINS"
                     "OR BARBERSHOP WISEGUYS"
but you can boast of
the glazier's craft too
the adolescent copse still gets its kicks out of me
so raise the shutters
a house that dozed off in the rain
lo! the Carmelite friars coming with brass bands
                Ahhhhhh
Proletarians! you've nothing to lose but your chains,
          the world to win instead
priests generals conductors landladies nobody should set their teeth
on the night-table
willpower spurting up
I'm thinking of Momma too
an elephant took off in a wide curve from the Eiffel Tower on the right
the blind accordionist has put his soul out in the sun
mind you I'm the hero who gobbles his kids
and the unhappy are happiest
a jerk tried making a silk purse out of a sow's ear and shredded his fingers
off


avoid the jackasses with flowery backsides and the gorgeous gals
words aren't for carrying loads like stevedores
yet the poet can stand bravely on his head once death comes for us
but true it is that death is zilch
hangmen are fond of the warm hearth
and the most tragic thing in life
is a straight line

Through the drought we flew now we're singing of April
        showers and new leaves to Man
turning our faces at last to the sun to be unfolded we're
        trees we're stones
we're seas we have millions of children
the big talker's a small doer it's sad there are some magpie-
        birds living in each of us
we must create to live if we're to create we must set up
a druggist's balance in our hearts
1-2-3 for sure it all depends on general formulas
oh brother you who live in factories and workshops you who
break iron for bread
think of me without bread or iron
it's day the sky sleeping in black ashes over me
who hears my bell pealing from time to time
everything's in vain I stand before shut gates stars falling
        from my eyes
the glass shards of my hurts still scatter up on the wind
        sometimes but there's a full glass of water in my hands
I know that tonight the girl dies in her white slip
oh god oh god it's our fate
the sky sleeping
girl dying
we singing April showers and iron-green to people

morning trumpets hail us the elders and children of the
  morning
the serpent drops into our cold shadows before it can lift
  its eyes to us
remember me if I go water crinkles after my footsteps
now I'm at work among the four walls with pen brush chisel
  and other simple tools
there's fire and a secret unopened in my fingers I declare the
  rules of construction
but unfortunately we've to remake even our dearest friends'
  minds
I'm carbide lamp and miner in one what is it you can't
  understand about me
look here's the dish I made of white porcelain
the knife bloodied with the juice of the young fruit lies on it
don't laugh at me talking to you I can't break away from you
with your brave sons and fertile women
you're my life's springtime surroundings
my departure and my return
I bathe myself in light to be pure to smell good for you
a wave washes into the room to carry me off
I stand on a structure of iron
memories of your battles flower in my cry

rain falling over the land how sad this night dark great beast
    behind silver bars
a draught whistles in from the east and flags tighten their
    halyards shivering
these rainwhipped rags recall their glorious connections
    flags waving
from warriors' arms over the bleeding fields and smoking
    towns
odors suffocating stench and bonecutting cold
is it worth it to go on worth waiting idly
oh where's the grove where the wounded quarry may rest
    where's the spring from which lovers
take light into their dazzled eyes
in the next room someone's crying and I cover myself in
    vain her cry riddles the walls
I'd escape but the clouds blindfold me
I'd shout but the dawn comes up
If I could look out the window I'd see the curlyheaded
    child coming this way
on the path
I've no time to wait for him
I never mentioned it but you might have guessed
I'm condemned to die

ANNA KISS: born in 1939 in a hamlet. Kiss studied at Budapest University, and now teaches school in the capital. She has published nine volumes of poetry, including: *Fekete gyűrű / The Black Ring* (Szépirodalmi, 1974); *Kisertenek / I'm Haunted* (Szépirodalmi, 1976); *Vilagok / Worlds* (poems and plays, Szépirodalmi, 1978); *Tükörképek / Mirror Pictures* (prose poems, Mora, 1983); *A viszony / The Relationship* (Szépirodalmi, 1983).

# MINIATURES

Paper airplanes
flooding the road,
wind-up sparrows
on the branches:
death's flirting
again,
but gets nowhere
with me.

This mouth kisses
a wooden sword,
and the wood's
smeared with rouge.
Eve stands in the mirror,
Adam is set on fire,
ragdolls come tumbling down:
the redemption text.
A caption.

Flat breasts,
drooping lily,
cockeyed violet eyes;
mice have nibbled the tip
of the Virgin's buttoned shoe.
The Devil's bowing
out of the picture,
a smoke of gold on his hump,
his place filled by absence;
in the left corner an idyll:
flies mating.
Warrior.
Walrus moustache,
gingerbread medals,
gouts of blood
from the punctured heart.
As on old Hungarian
coats-of-arms,
two sad angels are propping
the homecomer up.

Butterfly slippers,
flannel panties,
angora cats for company,
gay Tarot cards
clapping out:
Thief's on his way
to this house.
Let the rascal come!
Hasn't the foggiest
what he's getting into!

The vile seducer
and the mature maiden.
Click! go her eyes
like a sleeping doll's,
and what can,
bulges.
A plump finger beckons
the rakish bachelor,
who seems unable
to tear himself from the posters on the kiosk.

The veteran's
all set
to mix gunpowder
with sausage drippings
to lure the kid's ghost
out of its pit
but the pit's empty,
although a cavalryman's huge moustache
blooms on the face
of the moon.
The Devil only knows
what's in vogue now.
Ibronka burns
the secret sign
between her breasts.
Thrice she tears
the grass of oblivion
away,
but in vain —
she's about as much in love
as that highrise.

Oil paintings touching
in their idiocy
keep watch over
the inky-eared schoolmaster:
Please, no more "F's"
today,
and 1 X 1 = 1
sinks into oblivion,
God's got his eye
on the ruler too.

At the entrance
to the Buck movie house,
there's a hole
in the middle of the newspaper:
so the scalpers
are under surveillance.
Meantime, antique Colts
peep out of the left pockets
of jackets.

Maybe!
whispers
the basil-scented nonesuch
as she takes her leave.
The peacock plume
on her big hat
quivers sentimentally,
as herself goes trippingly
from heart to heart.
Making the butcher practically
shiver.

Cheek neatly fitted to cheek,
those were the lovely, pearly,
pearl-coupled days.
The clock on the wall's
ticking like someone
who's not going off.
The timed roses
drop
in bursts.

Every night
the narrow-gauge railroad's
taken over by thugs;
they rumble
around the terrified town
in squeals of steam,
and feed the boiler
from a great sack of nuts.
Crazy!

The fox,
pointing a comb
at the checkered waistcoat,
Whatever!
Place your hand
on your heart,
confess
the tears pouring
from each escapade!
It's raining, though,
out of the Amsterdam
Baedeker.
The wanderer
clings to his beard,
the bridge opens under him,
clouds roll in
on the Amstel —
Grandfather Rembrandt's
eiderdowns fiercely working
the fleamarket over.

Sir,
should the Devil touch
an appraiser's coatbutton,
would you say
that opal ring becomes
a redhaired lady?

When
this old roué
refers to me as a saintly woman,
one thing's certain:
he's been misbehaving.
Let the tailor's wife
bite solemnly
on her marzipan.
My dear, we are all
saintly women,
so let's polish away
at the brass doorknobs.

Ragdolls sitting
on the sumac,
dimes on their eyes,
glass hearts tinkling
on a thread;
death's changed
tactics.

The Devil's put an Angel
under the magnifying lens,
and can't believe
he sees
staring back at him
his very own powdered face.
Oh, says he, oh!
and this is
the whole story?
Shoo, go to hell!

# COSMIC TAPESTRY

A little woman looks out the window:
the penny-tree starts chinking
a little man looks out:
penny-tree penny-chinking woman
they say nothing about it to each other
because one's feeding the hawk
the other the pigeon
and the mountains are compressed
the mountains retreat
suns set and rise
suns set and rise
the living feed the living
life gives food to life
there's always some flesh on the fishbones
seeds don't spill through the basket
they sleep in the one common bed
at the one common table
they call each other rose, gillyflower
the moon's on the cool tower of their palace
on its ardent tower the sun
silver and gold
inside their tower walls
chrysalid-blue
beyond their tower walls
butterfly-wing-blue
only the penny-tree changes
quivering, changing back
changing and re-changing
changing and re-changing
when the little woman looks out:
the penny-tree starts chinking
when the little man looks out:
penny-tree penny-chinking woman
they say nothing about it to each other
because one of them's feeding the hawk
the other the pigeon

and mountains are compressed
mountains retreat
suns set and rise
suns set and rise

down turn the heavens, sunless
the sky below turns moonless down
the earth stands still above the skies
roots grow roots from roots
down begins to mirror up
a little woman looks out the window:
the penny-tree starts chinking
a little man looks out the window:
penny-tree penny-chinking woman
they say nothing about it to each other
because one's feeding the hawk
the other the pigeon
mountains retreat
mountains are compressed
but it cannot dawn
it cannot even
what was feeds what was
the dead giving the dead food
there's always some flesh on the fishbones
seeds don't spill through the basket
they sleep in the one common bed
they call each other rose, gillyflower
at the one common table
within their tower walls
the chrysalid darkness
beyond their tower walls
the butterfly-wing darkness
only the penny-tree changes
quivering, changing back
changing and re-changing
changing and re-changing
when the little woman looks out:
the penny-tree starts chinking
when the little man looks out:
penny-tree penny-chinking woman
they say nothing about it to each other
because one's feeding the hawk

the other the pigeon
mountains retreat
mountains are compressed
but it cannot dawn
it cannot even

the heavens mirror themselves turning
the sky below turning again
the hair's darkness stiffens downward
the sleeve flares downward
the penny-tree's chinking quivering playing
whatever is missing it seems is there
all of it playing it all
I bite off the thread, my lord
I consider the work complete

MIHÁLY LADÁNYI: 1934-1986. Ladányi was born in Dévaványa, and studied at Budapest University. He worked as a reader for the Szépirodalmi publishing house, was on the staff of the daily Magyar Nemzet, and worked as teacher and head of a cultural center. He was awarded the Attila József prize for poetry in 1963. His published poetry collections include: *Az út kezdete / The Beginning of the Way* (1959); *Öklök és tenyerek / Hands and Fists* (1961); *Mint a madarak / Like Birds* (1963); *Utánad kószálok / I Wander After You* (1965); *Dobszóló / Drum Solo* (1967); *A túlodalon / Across the Street* (1969); *Élhettem volna gyönyörűen / I Could Have Lived so Nicely* (selected poems, 1970); *Kedvesebb hazát / A Dearer Homeland* (1971); *Seregek mögött / Behind the Armies* (selected poems, 1976); *Van időd / There's Still Time,* his 12th volume, appeared in 1985.

# FOR EXAMPLE

Adolescents
begin with poems
and go on to war,
they've scarcely time
to glance round in themselves,
not even the promising possibility of a mistake interests
them,
nor the fact that something unforeseen and
extraordinary
could happen to them.
For example, that they can get away with both.


# THREE DRAWINGS

The smell is tree blood. Tonight
the whole forest slashed its veins;
the deer wept.

Before me an ant drags itself through the dust,
carting a crumb from my supper —
out of joy one day I shall too.

Looking at the trees, I'm stunned by compassion;
scarred, they implore heaven
for a bird's nest.

# NO DENYING

I lived at a time when
> poets had descended Parnassus
> and businessmen
> were junketing up to Parnassus.
In the era of the hiss I went round yelling *ed vivat!*
> and so led my rude life —
> beauty's drifting man.
I hated that bum's getup, but anyhow
> the wind could drench me, and
> I could feel free again, a sailor.

When moonlight wavered over the tiled roofs
> and paused on the bleared walls
> and I floated along between windows,
> my heart turned like a crazy compass.
Sighs echoing from those windows
seemed the Sirens singing enchantingly —
what can I say? I think there's no denying
I too might have been nominated
> President of the Poets' Chapter . . .
but at that time I could live on bread and
baconfat,
> besides, my poor love
> would have seemed awkward
> in the glare of the spotlight with me.
So, we never aimed to augment our glory,
> and we felt quite okay in this dazzling
> nothingness.

Loitering along those obscure streets
> we were greeted
> and they nodded back
> if we nodded at them first.
I sang them my song:
> and people sometimes said:
> "Oh, let Ladányi scribble his anarchist
> > doggerel . . ."

On we wandered, anxious too,
> scared that one fine day
> even that society might drop off astern . . .

We kept warm, curled up nights in close alleys
        like varmints scared by winter's onset
while hockshops bid
        for our ratty things
and our bundle of books dribbled back to the used
                                        shelf,
though by the time the cash came through
        night had long been there
        and all the stores were shut.
At those hours I wrote my poems,
        defiant, on fire,
        dreaming through the famished darkness
In the City of Clever Concerns —
        beauty's drifter.


## QUIETUDE


Hundred-year old flies sit
on the pot's chipped rim,
in which heavy hands
stir thin tales:

the time's coming
when kettles all are common,
and one won't be impaled
though one's hurt not even a fly —

hundred-year old flies sit
on the pot's chipped rim,
scratching at leisure. . .
everything's so far away.

# SKETCHBOOK

ENTRANCE
Last night the tales died
and there are neither stars nor dreams.
Two times two is four sings the king's camp,
boozing and clinking coins.

PHALANSTERY
Over the cities evening spreads desire
with its great, cool wings,
and there's nobody not dreaming of money
behind his bolted door.

BUSINESS
House and homeland they buy, selling dreams —
I offer their world for sale in my work.
I am faithful thus to the epoch of merchandisers.
A few volumes of poems are my ledgers.

ÁGNES NEMES NAGY: born 1922, Budapest. Studied Hungarian, Latin and art history at Budapest University, for some time on the staff of an educational magazine, taught secondary school for years before devoting herself entirely to writing. Translated works of Corneille, Racine, Molière, Brecht, Rilke, St. John Perse, and other English, French, German poets, both classical and modern. *A lovak és az angyalok / Horses and Angels* (selected poems, 1969). *Hatvannégy hattyú/ Sixty-Four Swans* (essays, Magvető, 1975). *Között / Between* (poems, Magvető, 1981); *Metszetek / Etchings* (essays, Magvető, 1982); *A hegyi költő / The Mountain Poet* (biography, Magvető, 1984); *Selected Poems* published by University of Iowa Press (1980). *Ehnaton* appeared in Journal des Poètes in Brussels (1980).

# CONSCIOUSNESS

Do I wake up, or lie here torpid
in this sultry, early summer heat?
The world bursts in wide strips
behind my brow — sunlight, sidewalks, trees —
and shreds the mist around me.

Should I wake from the shadowed droning?
Must I get up behind my blinds?
And what is there to say? What could this forehead do,
this rounded bone more precious than anything,
when everything that makes me me is dying?

It can't be helped. I want to think,
but pain holds me back from thinking,
because decay sprouts hour after hour,
and my thoughts, my hair, my fingers drop
like petals from a flower.

A leprous flower. I was not born sickly,
though cell by cell I'm eaten by rot.
How to put it? My brain remembers,
where this host of hidden roots
digs deeply into stronger ground.

The warm, fleshy petals fall,
everything sweet and mortal drops away;
desire remains, desire lives on like a thin, dry stalk;
in this shorn brain, my road, memory and will
return again: a forest that cannot be felled.

# SNOW

I
Silence pelting down
Is it something I'm hearing
this snow-white murkiness
Is it something I'm seeing

Only the pine only the roof
the edge on which it drops
as on the rim of things
growing brighter where it stops

II
Slantwise on the very edge
as on the peaks of things
just as in a strait passage
descending descending materializing

III
Like something readied long ago
like something waiting till this day
it's falling like something definite
on seasons that melt away

LÁSZLÓ NAGY: 1925-1981. Nagy was born in Felsőiszkáz, Western Hungary. Between 1946-1949 he studied painting, and attended a few terms at the University of Budapest as a member of the People's College Movement. Between 1949-52 he lived in Bulgaria on a state scholarship while editing an illustrated children's paper. His entire work — poems and translations — appeared in four volumes in 1975. Nagy's translations include folk poetry from Balkan countries, notably Yugoslavia, Bulgaria, Albania; the eastern Finno-Ugric peoples, and songs from Hungarian Gypsies. He also translated work by Robert Burns, Garcia Lorca, and Dylan Thomas. A volume of Nagy's selected poems was translated into English by Tony Connor and Kenneth McRobbie, and was called *Love of the Scorching Wind*, Oxford University Press, 1973. *Jönnek a harangok értem* / *The Bells Are Calling for Me* was his last collection, posthumously published in 1980.

# A HEADBOARD TO HEADBOARDS

On flower-lathered, green horses:
on the gravesigns of gravemounds, gravestones,
strange, heroic idols ride,
loyal horsemen standing in the stirrups.
Below the hoop of the sky and in my head,
where are those many, helmeted, veiled, ornate figures
driving to, and where do they arrive?
As if they're hauling this flickering star of mud,
this global human circus,
as if elsewhere there might be some
hope, in some other magnetic belt,
as if what is not here were there.
Every space in the world is furnished
with fire and ice, but not with what's needed.
Where is it, if not in making-believe,
where, you headboarded hosts of graveyards?
It's a shame, a shame, you gallop
all weaponless, faith and saga in rags,
round your sidereal orbit into the
streaming arrows of radiation, into the armies
of frost, to crash, and collapse.
My skull's listening: fiber parts from fiber
and your globe-heads split,
your tulip-heads, rose- and star-peaks
fall, and your hearts, worn outside,
are torn — woe to you, naïfs!
You don't flourish star-cloaks,
your train is memory and fine superstition:
how much blood, how many weddings, vintages,
master's whipping posts, rope's blue welts,
master's spittle, but, radiating neatness,
miracle and invention, how much black
and white mourning you tow through
the tolling of time, how many weeping miseries,
swooning spouses, how much darkness of death
embroidered with candlelight,
that stubborn, enthusiastic, man-evoking, peacock-eyed
flame — and how many gifts shine and rot
while your green horses ride on, but still,

hurrah for fine superstition!
To those believed yet living, the living
bring whatever they were so fond of:
a toy, candy, a doll, a jellyapple,
the best cut, fine wine, it's not rude to take a sip,
and it's mannerly to wear a silk ribbon,
a wedding shirt in the snow, and, even if it's freezing,
my shoulder doesn't shiver, nor does my chiselled
rope of an eyebrow — fainting into lovely
superstition I change, persecuted, an ax-carved,
oaktree-lad, coalblack boots burned on me by flame,
dark complexion smeared on me with vinegared
iron dust, mirror-brightened by bull's liver. . . .
A headboard to headboards, I gallop along
with your good army, a flagstaff
bored into my pate, its banner snowy cambric,
and words poured over my chest in red wine,
fish-scale cash silvering my steed's breast,
I ride for what's missing,
making-believe, never scared,
though wounded, punctured
with butterfly-hatching cracks, toting
a swan's egg of snow in a hollow,
faithful to myself, though I'm mossy
on my north side, and faded on the south.
Leaving behind my acids, my salts, my lovely shoulder;
aching humanly:
for my share, for the best of me, riding
mutilated through this world that's weeping with
emptiness,
that was meant to be whole.

# COGNITION, LANGUAGE, POETRY

Let's not be ruthless to ourselves: we must
not condemn humanity to the infinite. Full
cognition is in itself infinite. — If I
thought I was arguing against action,
I'd be praying through livid lips; in fact,
it's from the very first that I went after
this agony, the essentially human. Creature
of action even then, from the moment the
first word was shaped, a poet and scientist
both.

Heisenberg's formula for the world is lovely,
because radiating at me from it are the
strikers of fire, casters of bronze,
seafarers, stargazers, and bloodypinioned
Icaruses too, fierytongued heretics,
mouthcrushed singers.

They chatter on about describing the world,
expressing it. I don't believe the goal
is happiness. Science was here in the very
act of cognition even before the human word.
Still, poets haven't just clambered down
out of the trees either. Eddington's
dinnertable, the apparent one and the real
one, is made by the poet. And the woman
in Attila József's "Ode"[1] isn't just an
anatomical marvel in verse form. Without
the word, nothing occurs. Thinking, they
say, the act of imaging and of equating,
originates in the brain linguistically.

The abuse of words is no modern conceit,
but it's more spectacular and distressing
than ever before. We see language being
used for eyewash, for lies. No wonder
people turn away from the vital questions;
all right if it's towards amusement; but
if towards wordlessness, then it hurts. The

philosophy of silence wasn't made up yesterday.
Csokonai[2] was also wounded by its barb, though
in vain; Rimbaud was whisked off forever
by its blackness. Silence is a comfortable
condition for me: a dead quiet. Bombast's
comfortable too, though immoral. What I'd
like is being the word's true champion.
If the Impossible's out of reach, let our
Fall at least be festive.

I'm grown up now and even the least of my
cells knows that the word and I are one
and the same thing. I think the poet's
revealed by his language. (Just as work,
even table manners, usually reveals the
Human.)

If the poet can be judged objectively, it
is by his poem. This certainty comforts
me: I believe in the word. My duty's
paying attention to the word. Handling
the word with care, devotion. I also believe
that it carries me beyond the locks to where
secrets wait for me alone. It takes me
to where the nonexistent begins. It leads
me along the edge of the bluff, always on
the lip of death.

[1] Attila József, the most famous poet of the 1930's. The "Ode" imaged a woman in
terms of machinery, somewhat in the manner, one might say, of a Leger painting.
[2] Csokonai (1773-1805), a neoClassical poet.

# HURRAH FOR TREES!

When the Faithless One gave me the cold
shoulder too, I found a hoarfrost bride,
a small birch on the hilltop, and my blood
didn't go black. But my mouth learned how
to murmur in the virgin frost. I'll return,
my beltwaisted, ringhanded one. Though
soon, when the Milky Way lit up for the
third time, looking like a woman on skis
a rose came gliding at me. This time I
don't cross the circle of my blindness towards
my old consolation. She can wait for me.
Because she knows nothing of love's duplicity,
such a bride's not furious, never throws
acid. Even now, in May, after twenty years,
if I went to see her with my jingling skin,
she'd give her silvery green blood. I
need a green-ceilinged clinic. Cure me!
you white-as-snow, you birch physician-ladies,
you nurses. Tied up in ropes of
smoke, I crave trees. Soot-imps squat on
my snowy shirt. The black empire's spreading
inside too, allied with many other wicked
powers. I dream about trees. About towers
of blossoms — my shoulders are jumping
like a kid's at all the weddings! All the
blossom-Esthers, all the Sarahs, Marys,
Judiths of blossoms! And the King Solomon
of blossoms, Dániel Berzsenyi.[1] And those early
engaged, who froze early: Hölderlin-blossom,
Nijinski-blossom. Early on, trees
nursed me, accustomed me to the sky. I'm
piloting a live, sour-cherrywood plane;
shining its cherry blossom lights, it takes
off from the hillside. I'm soaring away
over the shaggyheaded wheat, until the power
purring through the craft's gnarled, twig-
fuselage is pumping through my heart too
in my play. Because I land on my knees
too beneath the domed willow when the grove

of poplars keels over in the blasting
thunderstorm. And I run crazy among the
hearts and alphabets on the trunks of the
good soldiers. I even see my own initials
on one prone silver soldier. Roots skywards,
and my throat throbbing as though it were
one of those naked heron necks. And my
breath shouting: The trees are dead! Over
there that evergreen sea's dying. I try
to blow the callous cement dust off the
forest of pines, and my hope's graying
ominously too: You, gray god glancing idly
down, tell me if I'll ever finish my work?
Green star of mine, go to sleep, put yourself
out forever. Who can it be, humming this
wicked lullaby to the little sphere? A
heart of concrete. T-squared blind architect.
Destroying terrorist. He's sending the saw
at my tree, my cosmic sister to whom my
adoring faithfulness has shackled me. A
horizontal destiny snarling at us. But,
with the dignity of those condemned to
execution, I shout: Hurrah for trees!

[1]Dániel Berzsenyi (1776-1836), poet of rural themes, often in Classical hexameter:
eclogues, elegies, Latin and Greek-modelled; from the country nobility.

# THE BELLS ARE CALLING FOR ME

Bells, bells — worms cannot touch their lips.
Bells can't be contaminated. The spasm
of a stroke doesn't shake them. Coronaries
don't kill them. Under sleeping stars and
tolling owls, the bells clang and shiver
on their crowns. Not the bells of poems,
those antique Schilleresque bronze helmets.
They came into the world, yet never grew
old. Real bells, born in Györ. They reached
the white tower by way of the hyacinthine
oxen's drool, on slow, wreathed wheels. So
that the tower might sound. The bells ring,
clang, pronouncing the unbounded poem of
time, keeping us from going crazy on its
wild track. They raise us from the mud,
marry the ragged imagination to the blue
bride, infinity. The bells lament, they
comfort. They advance on the tempest, boldly
striking the white heart of the hailstorm.
Sisters of the mothering marble breasts,
they give the soul sound to suck. From the
Mary-blue dawn's windows, between the platters
of hot ponds and the noon sun, through foliage
or the blouse of snow, whenever calm's needed.
There are no lonely bells, only lonely poets.

The bells converse over the seas. They rattle
lakes in Canada. Far off fellow-countrymen
are shaken beside dark firewalls supported
by whalebone. In remote, snowcovered camps
the bells hug tottering exiles. The bells
weep beneath the falling snow where frozen
boys were stacked on each other like firewood.
Bells, bells — they keep track of me, too.
The bells are calling for me.
Let's go, let's go with the sounding bell,
let's stroll home through the air. With
hair plighted on the lily, with a flogged
face, through smoke. Carefully stepping

on the crowns of poplars so the bird's nest
won't drip blood at our heels. I'm stepping
out for home. For tower and mother. I dare
to be reborn. Strewing my years from on
high. In the bell's sounding, in the blowing
wind, László's taking off his leather vest,
stripping his shirt, and his flesh. I hang
my mad, cracking Lear-face on an oak, like
a soldier's cartridge pouch. As a crib for
the thrumming, wild bees. To be rebuilt
with honeycomb chambers, filled up with honey,
honey. Because it's lost all its sweetness.
I'm not afraid of a sudden dwindling, not
afraid of annihilation. Because now I'm
light, I'm ozone, the stench of lightning
on stone. The star's distant stare, superstition,
moontide. I shine in my father's wine, I
live in mother's bread. Salt and vinegar
now, the small, willed whiteness of life.
A cellule as moved by a kiss as Attila with
his silver helmet and his whip, sentenced
to die at the head of his catkin-scented,
Milky Way Horde. But I reach my goal, I
win. The earth's quaking, the world's thundering
in my flesh. There inside, it's all mine.
I'm being constructed, getting set to be
flesh, bone, fist. I sally forth bloodied
on the damask mountain ranges. You're ugly,
ugly, ugly, they spit at me, the way they
do at the foal. And there I'm spilled out.
The merciless one, full of beauty. A red
thread round my wrist against the blight,
to keep the Woman who rustles through the
maize and smokes babies in a paunchy pipe
from taking me. The wheat's measured out
for the midwife so she can bake up a batch
of burning cakes and draw them like babies
out of the oven. I clasp the light of the
lamp, the sun, the moon, I yank my father's
hat off, pull my mother's hair. I persecute
them even in my dreaming, my fist coming
out of the swaddling clothes to clutch at

invisible reins. Their sinews are plucked,
their bones rattled. They are crippled.
Their knees wamble along through time. They
burn in the sun, drop in cindery sketchings
on the moon.

Earth: *ecce terra.* Am I gazing at it from
the surface or marveling from the skies?
From dust first, then from the tree, the
tower. Next from a rearing colt of a cloud
at the zenith, intending rain. Sitting on
a grain of dust suffices me, at the foot
of a sweet-scented stalk of dill, and now
I've a tree, land, a little horse, a little
plow, a little crop. But I'm growing up,
earth! To the blacksmith I take iron wings,
a colter. It goes red in the forge, is honed
on the anvil. I trudge in the track of a
wheeled, deadweight iron bird in the furrow.
Blossoms of stubble take a nosedive, alas.
And up come rustbitten rings, Pannonian trash,
rotten spokes and ringlets of fingers. Earth,
you vomit the spoons you swallowed. I drive
through nests of shrews and ant-castles.
Ping-pong balls: lively lizard eggs lashing
my ankles. The hare bounds from me in its
piss-stained shorts — salt in its ear, pepper
in its eye — I call. But from its barley-gold coach
a chipmunk stares at me like a
landlord. And the bell starts tolling in
me. Earth, you humus, you gray clay you,
expressing and delivering blessing when you're
cultivated, sown humanly. Rows of fat vetch,
clover, and lucerne wallowing on you. Stacks
are your knots of hair, crops the great gold
crosses on your breast. You pour out corn,
potatoes, carrots and pumpkins. I sit below
the bridge and hear blessing rumbling over
me on wheels, horseshoes overhead. But earth,
you bleak, you stony bench of basking waters,
you pebblefield, you sandy plateau, bridgehead
of drought, where deaths march off in yellow

hats and trousers: to glean what green remains.
Earth, cultivated even under the surface
by unseen little creatures and ugly yet holy
worms, soft, silver-lipped worshippers, composters
of the soil. And ants, building always and
so often in vain. Seated atop Red Mound,
I reach out into the valley with tweezering
fingers, into the throngs, among ants: so,
this one's Uncle Miklosh, Aunt Julie, Aunt
Gisella, that's Imrush, busier than ants,
little Marishka, Ilushka. And these white
pupas? Babies the bustling, the work's all
for. How often they have to pray, to beseech!
When even the bells helplessly fight the
hail clouds. I snatch at ice on the ground,
the image of Mary's there, the saw runs,
like the blue forget-me-not in Carnival candy.[1]
But what I see's Haynau Zapolya, the king,
with his crown and the rest of it.[2] Forget — me-
nots. Even the snake in the garden scarcely
disturbs a flower. But have you seen an
iron chain dragged across the gillyflowers?
I have, and there's no forgetting that! Hungary,
my wrath frames the image of your terrible
gardeners. I'll grow up too, flash across
their windows, my unshorn hair floating with
the moon, my horse leaving no hoofprints.
Although the spy, the dog, is onto my scent,
the cop's been hunting me a good long while.
I keep my vigil on the basalt hill. I drink
the star in the wine above the spring where
the amorous hops embrace. Keeping my vigil
at dawn too, I look at the verdant crop where
naked virgins following swine spread the
wide cambric to soak up the medicinal dew.[3]
Oh, if only superstition's mares, these women,
raw-green scented, would haul me along: I
could weep as clean as the suffering, wrung-out
cambric in the valley! Here are three
chapels: Margit, Ilona, Anna; with their
whiteness they cover the rascal. Slander,
envy, betrayal: if these don't ruin me, I'll

build churches atop the hill for other names
too, above the gold vines of the volcano.
You earth, what an illusion this world is!
I stroke and thwack the earth.

Doom-doom duh doomdoom, the contrabass grumps.
You must come for the bride before Lent.
They glide on sledges towards Zala over slush,
mouths stuffed with Carnival cakes. The
bridge's legs muddied, lace bloomers mudsplashed.
Because snow melts under the runners, my
Lord. The wedding guests trudge through
the slop. The tuft drops from the drooping
heads of the horses. The horses sticking
their tongues out, the only decoration displayed.
Doom-doom duh doomdoom, the contrabass grumps
when it's time for the key of flowers. The
little mutt scurries off into the grass with
the discarded moonblood napkin. The fly
flies doubled, a great green ticking in the
world. The lake swells, putting on a frog-spittled vest, a
green one, gold-enamelled
pocketwatch ding-dinging from how many pocketwatches
upon pocketwatches in its pockets. From
root to crown a string's stretched in the
tree, a string in the bird, a string in the
egg. A string in the boy who spurts his
sperm into a little jar he buries at the
foot of the cherry tree, maybe a drop of
blood will form there, maybe it'll sprout!
Chicks will hatch beneath the shaky beds.
The hen brooding in her basket knocks her
knot of hair awry in her stupor, the bed
creaks because its legs are rosemary, its
legs. The girls whitewash the stable into
a white palace, they scrub, they wash with
tiny hands, and curtains will be wafting
on what were once the piglets' windows. The
sofa's hemlock-leaf, lacy green all over —
there we lie, but the old ones thrust us
out of Eden, making room for Yorkshire hogs!
Girls, girls, the dearly clumsy potato-Madonna.

But ringed fingers grab it, breaking off
the baby's head. Why on earth have so many
bad children, whatever for! There should
instead be plenty of peas, poppy and cereals.
Chicken, goose, duck, pigs innumerable. Horse's
brat, cow's brat. On with them, on with
them — after which man's brat may breed.
Oh even the bells are astonished, oh. And
doom-doom duh doomdoom, the contrabass grumps.
Long live stallions, bulls, billy goats,
rams, cocks! Long live cows, heifers, mares,
sows, hens, ewes! Long live pairing, mounting,
covering! Long live littering! Long live
the Crop! Excited, kids lie on rabbits,
kissing the wheat's tiny genitalia. And
scratching signs into the great pumpkin,
and shoving at it, tossing it like a Willendorf
Venus, oh doom-doom duh doomdoom, the contrabass
barrenly grumps. I chop the cradle to pieces
in my fury, yet come alive in its ashes.
In the bells' Sunday pealing, I'm joined
to my mate on the needlegrass-covered hill
and we go rolling down to the valley, moaning,
quivering, whinnying in public. Doom-doom
duh doomdoom, the contrabass grumps amazed.
The Boba Gypsies play it beneath a fraying
tent. The contrabass shakes the dust beside
the cemetery. As though a slanted headstone
had been strung for today. The dance in
the dust goes slowly, like an old man. Though
bitter. The beer's tepid, the wine's mean,
but you can get drunk. Pursing his lips,
he sighs, pondering — the words come faster
then: my dear Latzi, my dear gentleman friend,
are you enjoying the Fels-Felsöiszkas Fair?

Earth, where fate equipped our parents for
one mortal dash. The snow melts on their
backs and by summer their skin clatters.
The butterfly can't crouch on them, the bird
can't cry for them, they hear only insect
music and the screek of their sinister stars.

Head first they sprint against spinning clouds
of gnats, beetles run into the juice of their
eyes, their foreheads are ruined by frost.
They stub their toes on stones, they walk
into thistle, on snakebones. They hop on
one foot, ludicrous, lamentable. They crawl
on their knees, on all fours, competing at
gathering potatoes. They run with bag, basket,
hurricane lamp, nostrum. The hat has to
be held in the wind, the swan's egg of the
ruptured belly's crust has to be crammed
back in with a fist. They trample the stack
underfoot, panting — and the household cold
clay, their legs attracting the spasm's glittering
grip of iron. Our parents are muddy, full
of chaff, stained by offal and must. They
bend to tie up the green shoots, how they
thump. Their bundle of raffia hisses to
the ground: horsetail at their buttocks.
Their clothes the blue of copper sulfate,
feet the green of May's dung juice. Out
of the polliniferous fields they come in
boots gold to the knees. Bloodstained to
the elbows at pigkilling. Limewhite at limeslaking
as the Angels of the Lord in Sodom and Gomorrah,
averting their faces from the seething. Walking
veiled in mulberry-blue when the erysipelas
epidemic is raging. Red with anger. Black
with debt. What's heaven like? They steep
camomile tea there, roast barley to have
malt for coffee. There my father chainsmokes
Herzogovina cigarettes.[4] We float on the
smoke of marbled whorls. Arm in arm the
paired parents walk. There's a board made
of cornflower in the pan, a golden-panelled
icon-face, my mother's, in the silver of
sugar, ruby of grape. Heaven is the scent
of pine, the Christmas tree in its mangelwurzel
stand. Figures hang there, the cookie dolls,
the edible timepiece, the boot, the embroidered
rooster and gaudy hussar. The stage is lit,
my sister in white stockings jumps from

heaven, her crepe wings useless to her, her
legs give way, never mind, she crawls from
the stage, her this-worldly panties flashing.
Garden of Eden, I'm dazzled into the infinite
when my face nuzzles the rose. After lunch,
when blood descends from the brain and my
viscera thrive, I lie down on a bed of gillyflowers.
A flower's there: its stirring stigma are
nails and a little mallet poises over them:
the Golgotha flower. And Palm Sunday's a
horror: I go ahead between windows on the
stubborn donkey of my blood and glimpse my
beat-up face in the mirror, my present and
my future. That's how you end up — a voice
says — when you try to do better, if your
taste's superhuman. Black-and-blue marks —
that's your field of violets. — A souvenir
of hell, a souvenir — the devil cries, and
my heart's on a string, sleazy with dread.
I'm translating the signs so you'll know
what I've lived through: I'm lying in the
manger, rats slipping from my drowsy lips,
dropping in my ear because they're also dribbling
from the horse's upturned muzzle more terribly
than glanders. And the horse's hide is on
the scales, only his tail hanging into the
pantry's dust, over him five bitter wounds
on the crosses in the breadboard. And I
tell you that you may know, my mother runs
from the naked weapon in thunderbolts up
to the tower, puts on the bell, the bell
with Mary, terrified. In the bell's pealing,
I pick her hair out of the splintered boards
of floor and lathing. And my mother's the
bell at my sickbed, above the eiderdown,
feverish, in hot weather and the Dog Days —
but she too drops at midnight, only Mr. Spielman's
tractors hammering like the devil at my eardrums.
I go on resolving the devil's hellish embellishments
because my father and mother are rummaging
ruffled like the stomach of a hog dead of
swine fever: the carmine fat, the black violet

loops of bowel, the fetid floating hoopskirt's
net! The fata morgana of danger quivers
in the air because a puppet theater stands
in every threshing yard, because hands are
dressed, dressed in pestilential ruffles.
And the dancing and shrieking's loud: cops
beating up on gypsies in the Culture Center
for being apostles of pestilence — who merely
wanted something to eat. We reek of carcass
fat, we make soap.. Hellish soap, our cheeks
and hands aching from its granules, the water
rosy in the poplar basin, in the bowl.
Dearest, hell's here on earth, but heaven is nowhere —
says a prince degraded into a drover who'd
give four bits for my whip. Who then boils
like rage in the devil's or god's iron pan?
Only us, all kith and kin! Our hands in
the air, parents' the highest: the callused,
the chapped, the dulled by soil, marred by
lye, by soda ash, the eagle-clawed and
the thorn-scarred, the throbbing, the hilly,
the ditchy, the streamy, moony, starry —
the hands of a sorry atlas of the world.

*Oragna figa marina gaminafa* — Mozart's not
making music here, but calling for me like
the Others, because they whispered in one
another's ear and I was led away from the
grasses of the Barbarians. Mozart's not
making music here, I'm just catching his
childlike image on the wind, from the droning
cicadas. Because it floats there before
me, descends, rises again, and would wing
along like a delusory bird — paper's a little
bird. I press its creases with my pinky,
lo, a doll with hair, death standing behind
him and turning the leaves of music. But
he's watching me alone. I also stare at him
with the calves. We read his sweet, milky-
pearly composition, the original one: *o-
ragna figa taxa- fa ma- rina ga- minafa.* The
wind can't carry it anymore. I fold it like

a wing, hide it in my satchel. I collect
wings and don't even know I'm collecting wings.
They're white, black, angelic, demonic. Wings
of the skylark who crashes into my aimless
slingshot to make me sob so that sorrow and
grief should also give me wings. Why do
I wade in the ryefield soaked to my chin
with dew? Putting on weight, why do I rummage
through cradles in corners for blister-beetles? Why
do I gather diamond-green ashflies —
teeming, fetid hell in a jar? To buy paints
with them so that the wings of color might
be mine too. To paint me a peacock, a mare,
and Ferenc Rákoczi with a flag. To become
a student. Behind me the bells, encouraging
me, supporting me with their foreheads like
bison. Forward, only forward, bravely. And
why did I have to see that dead girl? Whom
the midwives put away with her baby, away
into death? Whom the expert white team's
dissecting in the locked cartshed. The bells
go mad too while I watch it through the crack
in the attic, while the bloodpoisoned body's
dressed like a bride and the depraved dear
forehead's bound with the myrtle wreath.
The Magdalen-black wings will carry me. Because
I, I alone undertake her as a bride. We
fly, but below the earth, in the netherworld,
my mate, my country with a black womb, black
veins. Magdalen, Magdalen. Magdalen wanted
to live. A crag, a crag it is with liongrass
where I turn and turn in love and wrath,
revolving around a herdsman's whip, weeping,
losing weight, without food, thirsty, day
and night unceasingly. I make my halo from
a thunderbolt while my ears go deaf and the
forest's green ears are splitting, the birds'
eggs shattering, while Ság Hill sunders before
me and Dániel, the poet,[5] steps forth,
opens his book, it's white as winter,
and hands me his snow wings: the brown brows
of his Lolly.

My mother's washing my hair - washing it
for the last time - with lye made of aspen
ashes so that my head will ring like silver,
like the aspen's silver matting. For the
last time she's ironing my shirt too, and
now I'm saying goodbye. Farewell, you inner
recesses furred with autumn's flies, stable-and
kitchenwalls. I'm passing now beyond
even the vaulted corridors of schools, on
a flinty-odored journey even longer than
the roads . . . *ma- rina ga- minafa*. . . . I forget
the words. Call for me now, bells.

¹Usually made specially for Carnivaltime.
²Haynau Zápolya, a Hungarian ruler of questionable reputation during the Turkish
Conquest of the 16th Century.
³A still-persistent folk practice.
⁴"Herzogovina" cigarettes were the cheapest grade of tobacco during World War I.
⁵Dániel Bersenyi (1776-1836), poet of rural themes in Classical hexameter: eclogues,
elegies and so forth. "Latzi" is the poet's nickname, "Laci" in Hungarian orthography.

# THE LITTLE JESUS OF THE BARREN

"Stay here with us, you can have our name, be our son." Then
what's left for Mother? And what good's a rotten egg to you?
The archpriest just told me I'm headed for reform school, to
the gallows, where the buzzards will get me. Because just as
the churchbell rang at noon I went under in the pond, because
that's how bad I am, fit only for burning. "You're the best,
the most beautiful in the whole world." Still, I can't be
yours. "You'll lie on the shepherd's sheepskin cape, on the
black side in the daytime, on the flower-stitched one at
night." It's full of fleas. "Aunt will give you sugared milk
in a goldrimmed glass with flowers on it." Why do they call
you seedless? "We have no acorn tree, and no acorns; that's
why we're seedless," Aunt sadly murmurs. "The seedless are
barren, like Rosie in the stall: she has no issue, no heifer,
no bullock," Uncle explains. Silence. Only the green acacia
foams in the fire, weeping. And I'm standing stark naked on
the stool. Even my little cock wakes, warmed by the fire's
halo. A little while ago I stood on the ice in the middle of
the pond as though on a little lace doily. Now bits and
pieces of me on the clothesline, my shirtsleeve dripping
tears. I'm bad, fit only for burning. Hell is fire too. If
I were to be cast on it, green, oh, I'm nearly drowned in
flames now. But Uncle takes the golden chain of song between
his teeth, shakes it till it rings, and bids me follow. My
chain, small as it is, rings sharply between my teeth. We
sing as if we're shoving our way through snowdrifts. . . . I
wait naked for my aunt to find something that fits me, but no.
She lays me in the chimney-corner, on the black side of the
sheepskin cloak, and sinks me under an eider bolster. They
presume I'm asleep, but beneath my eyelids I watch the fire
caressing the Christmas tree and two happy faces. Daytime's
twilight here, because the window's as tiny as a storm
lantern's. And the house is small too. And Uncle's big; when
his hat's on his head he can't stand up. The legs of his
boots are long too, not to mention his arms! He slings a
stone over the top of the church spire. He rips the air apart
when he sows, the seeds shrill from his fist with the sweep of
his swing. He'd sow the whole world, if it were his. But his
trouble's even bigger than he is. Because, when the fit's on

him he's like the tortured man in the Bible. No matter how
quietly he may be sitting, he's greased lightning when the
spasms come: he pulls the flower boxes down on him,
carnations, rosemary, passion flowers and gillyflowers. And
foams at the lips. But only he can tell a story out of the
big picture book. Yesterday we finished the Battle of
Branyiszko in a blizzard.[1] Pointing at the Christmas tree, I
begin to speak: that pastry-pipe's like the bangle on Pajko's
brow. "Gee!" says Uncle. That tinsel's the snail spit on the
wall of the cellar when the sun hits it. "Bejeez!" Uncle
slaps his knees. I can't find a simile for the sword (there
is none). Angry, I shove aside the bolster and stand naked on
the sheepskin. "What do you think you're doing?" I'm
standing on top of the mountain! "It's all buried in snow
now!" Never mind! "What do you want?" And I shout, Give me
soldiers! "What kind?" Cavalry! "How many?" A zillion!
"Where is the enemy?" We'll find him! Uncle groans in
silence like the camel in the picture. But my aunt croons
like the dove's soft wings: "My little blossom, you're
fighting even at Christmas time, when there's supposed to be
peace?" Yes, I fight then too. Even then!

[1]Branyiszko: a mountain and the name of a pass in the easternmost range of the
Carpathians. In 1849, the rebels defended the pass and were trapped there in
the Battle of Branyiszko, where they were defeated and perished.

# HERE IS NO SOUTHERN ISLAND

The soul was cold, too; we headed south
like swallows flashing off,
tossing boiled wine down our gullets
from the mirror-well of our chromed bottle
against the going-blue; but icicled locomotives
rattled up from the South to confront us: we couldn't believe
the treachery of tomorrow's Southern Island;
shivering, we teased each other: what
machinery, what brandy-stills
could be scavenged from them, all those copper
pipes and rings — but finally
we saw the palms fettered with ice,
men wearing old women's scarves
to protect their ears, and the bird
of poets, the albatross, staggering towards us
in galoshes. . .and our souls simply turned back,
back into the sword blades of the North,
where winter's natural.

IMRE ORAVECZ: born in 1943. Oravecz graduated from Debrecen University, having specialized in English and German, and studied linguistics for a year at University of Illinois, Chicago Circle. In 1973 Oravecz was invited to the International Writing Program at the University of Iowa, and was a visiting Fulbright Lecturer at the University of California at Santa Barbara in 1985-1986. He currently works as a member of the staff of the Budapest literary weekly *Élet es irodálom*. His first volume of poems *Héj , Husk* was published in (1972), followed by *Egy földterület növénytakarójának változasa / Various Vegetation on a Piece of Land* (1979), *Máshogy mindenki mas / Otherwise We're All Different* (1979), *A hópik könyve, The Hopi Book*, (1982), and *Szeptember 1972 / September 1972,* (1987). He has translated poems by Frank O'Hara, Gary Snyder, Anselm Hollo, and Thomas Merton.

9:00 A.M.

Nine o'clock, the radios in the building have shut
up, the racket's died down, the door's stopped
slamming, the tramping's gone off, nothing's left to
be overheard, I sit beside the gasheater, opposite
the window in an armchair I always wanted to
have recovered because I hated its color, but it
doesn't matter anymore, the sun's glaring through
the pane, raising the temperature a lot inside, my
neck hurts, probably premature calcification, I lean
back, cross my right leg over my left, lay two
hands lightly along the armrests, shift around till I
find what's comfortable, I had a bad night, I saw a
living, transparent wall in my sleep, it was full of
veins and it was festering, I float in the light,
resting, trying to forget it, a shadow falling on me
now and then by the vapor floating up outside
from the vent, as though a cloudy veil crossed the
bright sky, behind me the bed unmade, breakfast
accessories, saucer cup knife spoon, on the folding
tray, letters, vase, calendar, lamp, medicaments,
paper, pictures of my son, on another armchair
coat cap sweater socks gloves scarf and whatever
clothes, on the carpet a pile of newspapers,
briefcase on the couch, watch, whiskbroom, belt,
handkerchief, scissors, string, glue, ignition key,
shoes in a corner, skiboots, kitty-corner in the
background books I'll never read on bookshelves, I
dragged myself to this room because of the cold, to
cut the cost of heating, I don't use the others, they
don't exist for me, except for the toilet, this is foyer,
bed-, living-room, and study too, I sleep here, eat
dress undress work, everything I need dumped in
these few square feet, utensils thoughts feelings
memories, I'd prefer not moving away from here,
I'd put in days and nights here, making a virtue
out of necessity here, and so getting used to what's
waiting for me, retreat, dwindling, disappearing,
because this is absolutely what old age without you
will be like, so shrunken, tight, pragmatic, so
prosaic.

# BY THEN YOU'D DRESSED

By then you'd dressed and come out of the toilet
where you were hiding from me and from yourself,
you stood there by the bed in the room, by that bed,
you were undeniably there, without makeup, in the
same oppressive space in which I was present too,
into which, when it became obvious the king was
naked, I was finally admitted, you stood around
helpless, at arms' length yet immensely far from me,
as I paced to and fro, upset, burdened by a sense of
futility and pointlessness, and was about to step
over to you to help you because you couldn't help
me, when surprisingly he spoke up, the bed's owner,
whom I hadn't forgotten but who, naturally enough,
was kept beyond the reach of my consciousness,
asking me if I'd like a glass of wine, yes, that's what
he asked, no doubt embarrassed, not for himself but
by the fib with which you'd denied his presence, and
I'd've been ashamed too were I in my shorts where
he was, but, for him to ask that when he could have
offered me whatever, a nail, some of the afterglow, a
stove or cupboard, but not simply a glass of wine,
because anything would have been more apt than
the liquid symbol of hospitality by which in that
situation he was not merely mocking hospitality but
demeaning its symbol too, and, though not caring to
comment on the proceedings in that bed before I'd
materialized, I could sense the symbolism in his
degradation of the symbol.

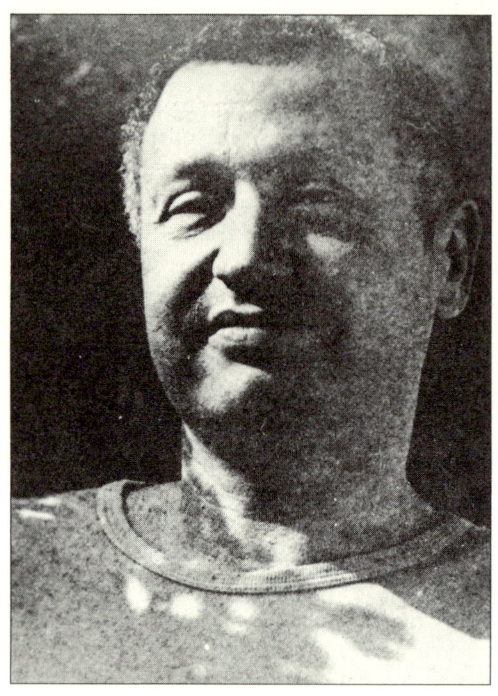

OTTÓ ORBÁN: born in 1936 in Budapest. His father was killed in a concentration camp; his childhood spent in a Budapest school for war orphans. Orbán studied Hungarian and English at the University of Budapest but left without a degree, and devoted himself to writing. He has published twelve collections, including: *Szegények lenni / Being Poor* (1974), *Távlat a történethoz / Perspective on the Story* (1976), and *Szép nyári nap . . . / A Lovely Summer Day . . .* (1984). His translations include a volume of selected poems and plays by Robert Lowell, and many American, English, French, German, Russian, Spanish poets, collected in *Aranygyapjú / Golden Fleece* (1972). Orban has traveled in France, Switzerland, England, Finland, the United States (where he was a guest of the Iowa International Writers Program), the USSR and India. His trip to India resulted in a volume of travel notes in prose. Orban also writes nursery rhymes, and *Helyzetünk az Óceánon / Our Bearings at Sea*, 111 prose poems arranged as "a novel-in-poems," published in 1983, represents yet another direction this brilliant stylist has taken.

# A SUMMER ON THE LAKE

The shore seemed suddenly more distant. Or had the other slid close?
It was nothing, though. They just climbed out. Picnicked on air mattresses.
As in the beginning, the dead sardines glistened
in the divine can's blued sauce. But on Earth's Screen
their broadcast destiny was visible only as a ghost. Location indeterminate,
outlines blurry: the fuzzed picture
of a time not past, nor future. Themselves and yet not. Nor was that sour taste
in their mouths from something more than they knew. Whatever could that have been?
Not even the paltry possibilities that had been theirs:
the same old streets, same old loves. They had lived where they
      could live;
and living from day to day is the same anywhere, isn't it? The
      portables
gushed their silent dance tunes. Illusory lives, glaring darkness.

Afterwards they chatted. Joking about — oh well, those! Yet their gossip
resurrected a heroic age out of their breasts, the downy gold
tingling along their thighs. And Tooth & Claw, Aphrodite of personal mythologies,
stands at the door again: "He could at least have had the decency not to phone
what it was like from my own bed!" The ashes-and-dust wagon
rattled along, accelerating. They slapped their thighs, haw haw haw.
Their kids dived off the landing; applause, kodak smiles
caught and fixed. Yes, it was they all right: who'd taught the frigid lady to enjoy
it and the nymphomaniacal model how to cook —
these commuters on a branchline to heaven. And love's inane, shiny, pharaonic
mask glowed defiantly
on their faces tilted sunward.
And then, shrieking, they were off on their way to Hotel Bones.

Behind them, worn out by leafing through the centuries,
the wind creaked an open window.

# CERTAIN YEARS

And down came years one after another
    like black clouds We might as well start like this
It's a straight line from here to poetry socalled
    His The-Beautiful-is-what-pleases-without-exciting-the-passions poem
sprinkled with a vision rising out of the kneadingtub
    and naturally a star's always welcome as a raisin
in the universal coffeecake for its light alone shining
    on the sentence Everything seems
Okay Image after image 100% of capacity
    And the city where I grew fearfully wise
emerging after the war Lips shut
    eloquent eyes No meat Mother coming home with an empty
shopping bag And in the pesticidal movie the newsreel's
    black-and-white dazzling with the future's Once-upon-a-time

It's easier this way Not raising the question
    are people to be blamed for what happens to them
And if they are because one way or another they are
    how and for how long? How big's the individual share of blame?
the collective? And where do the stories start?
    What conqueror wasn't conquered once?
And which of the conquered wouldn't prefer conquering?
    And who hasn't a good excuse for anything?
But if everything's merely a link in the chain reaching to the primordial cell
    what's this acrid flavor in my mouth? whose blood?

I recall I'd just stepped off the sidewalk The burst
    nearly flung me against the wall I saw his face
Like mine the scared face of a child He just hangs onto
    the machinegun and mows away Any set of years
anywhere You squeeze yourself into the future between two years
    the barking harrying your heels You know him that
improviser capable of the lesser of two evils
    or an inexplicable good His own prisoner To that extent free
Around the monkeyface blooming on the poster tacked to the Earth
    glory radiating everywhere

# REQUIEM

He tossed a life preserver to the young castaway in '55
a longish first translation job for the bedhopping ingenu
about this monster poem says he
*it's an epic shtick you can live off it meanwhile*
he'd remembered me as the precocious monkey

the years then
our years on earth
first shooting then silence is all it is up close everything
seems small time
but seen from a distance
as though one thumbed through Revelations
between a bloodypimpled sky and burning houses
we both aged
a pair of family men

I have my notion of Resurrection
the angel reeling off the official text
took me for someone else when
he pinned the brass medal to my rib

the afterlife 1964
raining windy
K's coming from the direction of the Tuileries
his sweater blooming as big as the Czar's Bell its hem
hanging on him like a skirt
he says let's sit down someplace before we freeze

Sainted Trinity of paupers
he Julie and I pooling our francs on payday
laughing as though we lived it up
and we are alive because we've invented immortality
(the kind we can afford)
a bottle of rosé

# THE FACE OF CREATION

I returned yet again to look Time in the eye the Seventies the old garden
      gone plaster peeling off the walls
the hectic valkyries of the technocratic opera leapfrogging
      on the runway
incredible that a real story with real characters should have
      happened here
and even more incredible the golden day of the country's postwar creativity
      and the foamy blue southern sky frothing from tree to tree
and I feel silly pressing my ghostmug into the rustbitten
      barbwire of the paradisaical lager and for a minute
        I feel like really dying seeing the path in the woods taking
        another turn and some of the dilapidated shanties torn down
it's incredible that all I so heartily hated
      could have grown splendid and sweet
for truly I betrayed them surviving them
to stand here in a time saturated with complex problems as
      an egghead on a TV quiz panel delivers the verdict on his
      fellow humans
but the Very Reverend's Missus's self-consuming ardor burns in my throat
      like·the glance of a pantherbride her passion
      once used to assess those neat American Mission GI's
      dashing about in their jeeps
and in the gasoline-reeking snow-movie it's not the Frozen Child
      who ascends to heaven on the ladder of transcendental light
but terrestrial electricity sparking between the poles of the world
poverty passions the poignant current of the human presence
no need asking with a mournful face where she ended up and
      whatever happened to her perfect form
I can see Spring blazing on the grass frozen to cotton and Uncle
      Mickey
      rolling naked on the ground
He's yelling at the clouds lipstick on his chest and blowing fire out of
      his mouth the flames of rotgut wine
and over there Saint Yolanda cutting across the yard Golgotha
      T-Square in hand
      her crown of hair armored against temptation
because Satan's skirt's rustling down the dorm corridor at night and the
      perfervid adolescents grapple one another in helpless cravings
wind and profoundest respiration WE LIVE

time to knead the dangerous masterpiece out of the clay
to listen to the arrhythmical panting the yowling ecstasy
        to roam over the skin twitching beneath her blouse
time to experience the frenzied instant of The Creation
this goes on till the end of day. . . JJ's a weakwilled
        female she's been laying herself down on her back at
                the merest
        sigh and spreading since she was 20
on the concrete floor of the hut designated Kindergarten
        sits on an enamelled potty saying cawwit instead of carrot
and the war actually only stops now when the true winner gives out
        with his inaugural speech
and the diamond blade of May glisters in the teeth of the piratical
        earth
I roamed among the trees and years I see myself in that fur hat
        hair curly and frostfingered there is no resurrection
and on the fields of wonder mass produced houses the dog of the
        pig in clover barking from the balconette
but blood flowing between the cells finds the general the glorious
        human relativity
perfect Humpty Dumpty Theorem tested by death and war
and does it matter who lives how long if it all hangs
        together
and who cares about being tuned-in turned-on hip cool with it
        and the scholastic bleating of statistics
I can see the face of the creation        In the star-scarred blackened grass
        kids' mugs gorging on stolen apples dirty words like flotsam on the happy
sea of their panting
and from the borderless dark Boche cursings and the sound of twigs
        snapping
but they just squat there gorging
and in the chicken-cackling, gunfire-crackling that fills the world
        they flick
        bugs off their legs and reveal their
        shiny sharp teeth
while the glory pours its rays down on their tousled heads from an
        indeterminate point-source
where finite and infinite converge and muscle contracts
        winging itself aloft now


Ottó Orbán / 109

JÁNOS PILINSZKY: born in 1921 in Budapest. Died in 1981. Pilinszky attended Budapest University but was drafted towards the end of World War II. He was taken to Germany, where he saw the concentration camps while making his way back to Hungary in 1945. His books include: *Nagyvárosi ikonok / Metropolitan Icons,* collected poems (1970); *Szálkák / Splinters,* poems (1972); *Kráter / Crater,* new and selected poems (Szepirodalmi 1976); *Beszelgetesek, Sheryl Sutonnal / Conversations with Sheryl Sutton,* verse novel (Szepirodalmi, 1977); *Válogatott művei / Selected Works,* poems, prose, drama (Magvető-Szépirodalmi, 1978); Szög és olaj / *Nail and Oil,* prose (Vigilia, 1982); and *A mélypont ünnepélye / In Praise of the Nadir,* prose (Szépirodalmi, 1984). Three volumes of selections have appeared in English; others in German, Norwegian, and Finnish.

# APOCRYPHA

I

Because everything will be deserted then.

The silence of lonely skies,
of sunken fields at the world's ending
and lonely kennels too.
Overhead a fleeing host of birds.
We will see the sun rise
mute as a mad eyeball,
placid as a crouching beast of prey.

Yet I keep vigil in my exile —
for on that night I cannot sleep —
Tossing, turning through the small hours
as the tree's thousand leaves speak:

Do you know the march of years
over the harrowed fields?

And do you understand mortal wrinkles,
do you know my horny hand?
and what it means to be orphaned?
and do you know what agony
walks this endless night
on cloven hooves, on webbed foot?
The night, the cold, the pit,
the prisoner's wrenched head:
do you know the stunned ditches,
the torture in the abyss?

The sun's up. Trees like sticks, black
against the the raging sky's infrared.

So I set out. A man walks in silence
across the face of desolation.
He has nothing but his shadow.
His stick. His prison clothes.

II
For this I learned to walk! For
these last, bitter steps.

Then twilight comes, and the night's mud
to turn me to stone, and through slitted lids
I stand sentry over this procession
of feverish shrubs and little twigs,
this tiny, hot forest, leaf by leaf.
This was once Paradise.
In half-sleep, the pain returns:
hear its great trees!

I wanted to make it home, home at last,
just as he returned in the Bible.
My ghastly shadow in the yard.
An exhausted silence, a house of old folks.
And here they come, poor things, calling me,
weeping, clumsily hugging me.
The ancient order takes me in.
I prop my elbows on the windy stars.

If only I could speak to you now,
whom I loved so much! All those years
I never stopped saying what a child sobs
through the palings, the choked-up hope
that I'd come back and find you.
Your closeness throbs in my throat.
I'm shy as a wild creature.

I do not speak your words,
human speech. Heartbroken birds
fleeing now
beneath the sky, the blazing sky.
Solitary stakes stand in a glowing meadow,
and unmoving, burning cages.
I do not comprehend human speech,
I do not talk your language.
My words are more homeless than the Word!
I have no words!

Its awful burden

tumbles down the air,
the tower's body sounding

You're nowhere. An empty world.
Deckchair, garden chair left outdoors.
My shadow clattering among sharp stones.
I'm tired. I stick out of the earth.

III
God sees me stand in the sun.
Sees my shadow on stone and fence.
Sees my shadow stand
breathless in the vacuum.

By then I'm turned to stone;
dead folds, a thousand etched grooves,
the faces of creatures no larger
than a handful of rubble by then.

And furrows on faces instead of tears,
trickling, the empty ditch trickling down.


# A MEDITATION


Is pariah art possible? Can that animal ataraxia
locked in Man hope for forms, words? Is just a
pulsing rhythm possible, like dogs in summertime?
A spirit poorer than any simile and stone bare, not
in consciousness but riveted to earth? Language
powerless to utter its foliage?

Because here's a thirst no one's offered a drink.
Worse than ever, the gasping bole of misery.

All power and glory to His will.


János Pilinszky / 113

# HARBACH 1944

Over and over I see them:
moonlight, a long pole,
and men yoked to that pole,
heaving at an enormous cart.

As night comes on;
the cart they haul grows huger
their bodies shared by dust,
hunger, and trembling.

They drag road, landscape,
freezing potato fields;
but the heavy landscape
most weighs them down.

They sway in their traces
each pressed against
another's frail form,
like living strata.

Villages make way for them,
and gates stand aside;
distance approaches,
staggers, and turns back.

They stumble on
with a dark clatter
of clogs as if wading
through ghostly, fallen leaves.

Their forms belong to silence now.
Their drawn faces lift
as though they scented
heaven's far-off manger.

And like a waiting,
empty fold that
shoves its gates apart,
death opens wide for them.

# THREE POEMS

*In Memoriam F. M. Dostoevsky*


Bow down. (Prostrates himself.)
Stand up. (Gets up.)
Remove your shirt and trousers.
(Takes them off.)
Look me in the eye.

(Turns away. Looks into the eyes.)
Get dressed.
(Puts his clothes on.)


STAVROGIN'S FAREWELL
"I'm bored. My cape, please.
Before you commit anything,
consider the rose garden,
single rose bush rather,
or one rose, gentlemen."


STAVROGIN'S RETURN
"You have not considered the rose garden,
and you've committed what is forbidden.

"From now on you shall be persecuted
and solitary, like the butterfly hunter.
Get under the glass, all of you.

"Under the glass, pinned by the point of the needle,
shining, a bivouac of butterflies shining.
You are shining, gentlemen.

"I'm frightened. My cape, please."


János Pilinszky / 115

# IN PRAISE OF THE LOWEST LINE

Who'd dare read in that
bloodsteamed sty?
And who'd dare take off, for anywhere,
when sunset fractures the fields,
the sky's at flood-tide,
and earth at the ebb?

Who'd dare halt,
eyes shut,
there at that lowest line,
where a hand always waves for the last time. . .
roof,
lovely face, or
only that hand, that nod, that gesture?

Who could sink
calmly into the dream
that breaks over childhood's sorrows,
lifting the sea to his face
like a handful of water.


# THE PASSION ACCORDING TO RAVENSBRÜCK

He steps out from the others,
halts in the square's silence,
prison uniform, convict's head
an image wavering on some screen.

He's horribly alone,
his pores visible,
all of him immense,
all of him so small.

And that's all. The rest,
the rest — just that he
forgot to cry out
before he crumpled to earth.

GYÖRGY RÁBA: born in 1924. Raba studied French and Italian at the University of Budapest, then worked as a secondary school teacher. He survived slavery in a forced labor battalion during World War II. Raba was a member of the Institute for Literature of the Hungarian Academy of Sciences until 1984, when he retired. His books include: *Idegen ünnepek / Holidays Abroad* (translations, Magvető, 1974); *Rovások / Runes* (poems, Magvető, 1980); *Próbaidő / Testing* (poems, Szépirodalmi, 1982); *Újes válogatótt versek / New and Selected Poems* (1982); and *Babits Mihály / Michael Babits* (biography, Gondolat, 1983).

# PREFACE TO DYING



I have heard about the Indian
who went back twice
to the rolling hills
peeled away the dawn's mist

and like a starling cracked with just a tap
the green husk of the almond that had opened for him once before
then he rolled about like a happy pup
tail-wagging shouting yes or no as he pleased
to the black-and-white world

I'm dying happy with my one life
thanking my star
I was born no barbarian but a free soul
the sun of Hellas and cloudless truth shining in my heart
I lived with human wits and not as a dumb brute
I knew that even salt turns sweet on the tongue
and familiar bitterness milder

Wonderful to soar on youth's wide wings
in the skies of upwelling life
wonderful to find in that panorama the source of the reed marsh
the cold water of life amongst slippery stones
Its book opened to me every morning
a pair of swallows chivvying the harrier
a forgotten old appletree carrying luscious fruit
wonderful having each day dawn
a witness to the wisdom of my bones dropped behind
in clearings the years made

I thank my star
I lived when Socrates was alive
but my name's at the summit my pure name
it is given to none but me
to reach it
and what my life has held apart
alpha and omega
crash closed behind me there


## EPOS


Saga in daylight wilderness
I said to them, Come
carry off my thirty beings
Dawn is blank
Standing in water to my sash
for years we adored houseposts
now let's stick the miles
into our boots like a dagger

The stones on my way the stones are sleeping
our world's ballast ready to take off
they're skipping stones on wild water
they huddle because it's getting cold colder
They crumble they molder
and the wind carving new faces
Only death's funny
and real
its saltshaker ribs
And legs swinging ahead starting out
ankles like the whirling necks of bottles
bare feet drumming the ice

scaly heels the stony foundation
ships stranded in mudshoals
so beautiful the sadness of desire
Like voyages in a docked liner
males silent utterly in naked female stones

And fleeter than whistling
the road rushing below me
tree-lined a caress smiling
at arm's length there
at the tip of the branch
you green life you must never go

Homeward the tang of earth on our palate
and banners
Each day booty
But the off limits coming too late each night
all the lamps going dark
only rain on my stony face
writing nothing on it anymore


## HIMALAYA DAYS


Gulliver by then perceived
he was trudging between mountainous men
and he could call to one
who'd tuck his cheeks into his collar
as though the frost of daybreak had breathed at him
the response if any is drowned in mist
and he could turn to the other and shout
to whom it would sound like chirping
well some voice from nature's choir
what's it to him
and though the echo-hunter
once flung away a score of nets
now even looking round is loathesome
the word goes numb on his lips
and contemplating his neighbor's pore
is an alpine trek for him
even if he gazes at nothing
hauling himself ahead
questioning stones
still Gulliver knows
he's lugging a legend along

# GOING ON TALKING

What tocsin's needed here
to calibrate a shadow at noon?
or after lightning, thunder's Didn't I tell you so!
and isn't it grand to be recognized safely
and meet me here on the island of myself

Why regale you with stories
of riding a winged steed
the horse is just a horizontal body galloping along
the horse is just a cart jouncing through potholes
only wings — feathered or light-metalled — could lift
the man still hunting yesterday today

Or of wandering heights
opening doors on things never before glimpsed
the nestling that flutters under my ribs
not a word of my scorched hair's stench
how I got to this place beneath the sun
by crawling on my belly . . . those intolerable flames

Suddenly breaking silence
the parched wood of heaven and earth crackling

words finding each other unforeseen
why mention
who awaited me murmuring what at the forest's fringe
this chronicle's flesh seared away by its fevers
in the grass a snail shell, vacated

A map of veins raised on my hands
look that's my territory
eyes fixed beneath tremulant lids
this my history
and the world stops
just where my foot stands
I say nothing about the once upon a time
but tell you only what you see
the rainbow's hues one by one

György Rába / 121

# MY FACES

Pebbles
at ebbtide numberless
you my faces

I picked one up
Its . . . crayon gloss
a balloon
bobbing all day
against billboard spectaculars
not a crack not a scratch on it
Who says
he knows how time's passing

Another
as its dream rolled
down the pool table of a vacant barroom
its name lost in a fogged ravine
and because it was grooved by a gun butt
cracks clotting its epidermis
The whole form's needed, though
the world entire

Then a third a fourth
a hail of stones stone faces
which one to be mine
Swollen in the brutal light
they appear suddenly against the sun's disk
occluding it briefly
a pair of fossils
from disparate eras
horizons sealed in them
sublime solar eclipse
Who recalls lamenting strata

As long as the sun shines we're human

# NIGHT MEETING

A hand
to the light
the body a stalk
Flesh
over the furrowed flesh summer leans
turning itself to loam
And the voice
travelling home
over lost roads
hope of the dragons of March
the immemorial smashes at the dams
flooding out a steppe an insane firmament
what was written smeared away a desert
what was granite atoms freed forever
nothingness absolute inscribed on the clod
chronicles of sweet water parched to salt
vanished navies splintered
golden ages nameless
etched fountains drowned in the flood
a one and only anthem drowning the world's body
and the sawteeth ruling over all
Stammering confronts the record of what is
And again the murmuring harbor-wavelets
. . . lully-lulling lully-lulling
at every moment the cradle breaching

# STUDY: A HAND

Demands nothing threatens nothing
five fingers curled
as it reaches
reaches for the sky's loving edge
still victorious over
this heavy world
its knuckles an ax striking
at the tangle of war commands
through crushing thickets
cutting a way through space
before the first day
after a genesis
by force alone
silence surrounds it
somewhere
a forlorn sickle rasping
a bell chiming
it stands based
on other brave bones
beaten into compost
a mace against the wall of night
the shadow of a spire

A hand, hands
who set them at the world

# THE GREEKS ARE BLINDING POLYPHEMUS

Because he's one-eyed
because he prefers a different snack for lunch
because he takes an unknown path
because he's a shepherd though born a locksmith
because he hasn't heard a phalakrokorax in days
because he listens to the singing present
because he builds nothing squats in his cave
because he builds a cave garnished with laurel curtains
legs knees falling in line
they lug a fiery pole
like stepping a mast into its socket
they pierce and bore into his eye
because its hole is the house of death

But novelty lives in him too
every living eye shines like the sun
and the death that renders rigid
his rock-ripping muscles
lives in everybody
the form of the present is as clear
as somebody rowing barehanded

and though tomorrow's melody enchants
it rains down enamelled flakes

Many men will sail from here
amazement will never end
the dialogue of but and because
how long will you listen
o lord of eternal waters

György Rába / 125

SÁNDOR RÁKOS: born in 1921 in Újféherto-Kálmánháza, in northeastern Hungary, son of a village teacher. Rákos studied economics in Budapest, then worked in various administrative, journalistic, and editorial jobs. His published works include: *Meztelen arc* / *Naked Face* (1971); *Az emlék jelene* / *Memory's Present* (1973); *Elforgó ég* / *The Sky Turns Away*, essays (Magvető, 1974); *Harc a madárral* / *Fighting the Bird*, poems (Magvető, 1980); *Társasmonológ* / *Soliloquy with Others*, poems (Szépirodalmi, 1982); and *A tűz kérlélese* / *Imploring Fire*, collected poems (Szépirodalmi, 1984). He also has translated Gilgamesh and other pieces of Mesopotamian poetry, and a volume of folk poems from the South Sea Islands.

# BEAR SONG

*A bear was shot in Zebegeny*
*some hundred meters off*
*the highway and tourist trail.*
*The dangerous animal*
*must have wandered here from*
*the Fatra Mountains.*
                    (News item)


TO THE HUNTER
In the end God alone knows —
and maybe He doesn't — who's in the right:
the famished critter, stomach rumbling
as he stalks his victim, or the innocent
prey that would have preferred
to stay alive.

TO THE BEAR
You wound up in the wrong place, Uncle Shaggy,
far from your snowtopped forests, your bilberry-, raspberry-
scented glades, the security
of your secret den. From a wilderness remote
from human voices you strayed here,
to this lead-hued boulder now your
monument between the asphalt's roaring cars and a footpath
noisy with children. May your death be properly
mourned as a hero's death, the martyrdom
of a wild, free son of the weeping wilderness.
An ending that pains me, because I think
your tragic offense was only that you wandered:
so death's merciful balm is best
(according to ursine poetics).
Consider what your lot
must otherwise have been.
I see you staggering across the ring
with beach balls and hoops, a clumsy
clown in a tacky blue weskit
and baggy trousers —
you, a bear-artist, with two left legs,
the helpless butt of slapstick gags and witless chortling,
bowing low at the climax,

thanking the gracious, gentle crowd
for having condescended to laugh at you.
Or, locked up in the zoo,
waiting for goggling visitors who get
their kicks by offering pity
and mocking the captive kings,
those caged, royal creatures!
Would you have wanted that,
just to stay alive?
Or, to have roamed for a time
free beneath an indifferent sky,
stabbed by pangs of hunger,
blind fury goading you
against everything — until
in your bestial ignorance of the law
or sin you slaughter someone,
and it's called murder.
This way's best by far:
dying innocent, you redeemed
those innocents who'd have died
horribly, killed by you!

TO THE ANIMAL LOVER
Fine, love animals, our childlike
kith, our helpless kin, but
not as people-proxies. Love
them, keeping this in mind:
human beings may
menace human life —
but a beast? No way!

# THREE DOSTOIEVSKIAN MASKS

*From Raskolnikov's diary*

                freedom won't be sweet for him         without us he can't exist

iced-in        a frosted globe        inside         everywhere        me at its core

suspicion        (just and unjust)         packs space about me

bars        represses        even me        in the frore globe frosted over inside

here I belong        in existence inexistent        following geometry's eternal law

Raskolnikov        hunted Raskolnikov        I'm Raskolnikov

compared to me you're midgets all        snoring shacked up with women and life
                still, superior midgets

nicknames you give things        buddies with monday and tuesday
                dorming with Kid Jesus

though nothing comes along        you're thinking about        what might
                turn you a profit

I look elsewhere        which sets me apart        which is why I murdered

antisocial, you think        just included you out        another angle another
                bearing another way

had we promptly clarified it        you'd have understood        as it is merely
                contempt

despise and envy you        you despise and envy me        but Porfiry appreciates me

        mih rof teews eb t'now modeerf        tsixe t'nac eh su tuohtiw

reversed speech        the hunted, delirious one        hunting himself for the
                hypocrite hunter

Sándor Rákos / 129

he's sniggering        I'm sniggering along        I cut it out        even his
                reflexes he forces on me

rubberball Porfiry        with his orbital rationale        surrounding me everywhe
                bouncing,        caroming off my walls

playing fresh        mocking me        how long shall I take it        a conceited shi
                what I am


        mih rof tweews eb t'won modeerf        tsixe t'nac eh su tuohtiw


jumps in its catch        isn't locked they're rattling it        hook's hopping out
                I'm behind the door        up against the wall hiding flattened

my tongue by words        like the latch by two intruders        jaw slackens
                I'm behind the door        hiding my ideas

I said it        they got just the secondary, tertiary senses        I'm free for now

they'll discover anyway I was pure even after *that*        and won't forgive me for
                I'm sweat soaked now

Sonia        appears before me        backing up the stairs        just ahead of m

I'm blocked in by the place        a dog's howling        a woman heaves a rollingp
                at him

I'd like to get a hold on something        the wall shoves me away        on, on
                to confront Lieutenant Gunpowder        Give yourself up

vacant fireplace flues        sucking you to hell        Clear out of this, Sonia
                pointless, our sacrifice

and again Porfiry drops by        on the tip of his tongue he's already got
                my innocence

heaving a sigh        relieved sigh        this is what's really awful now
                I've grown into it

like I wanted to molt my hide          I can't just walk way from the hunt
     the heat's finally off          when Rodion Romanovich          you're the killer


          *freedom won't be sweet for him*          *without us he can't exist*

up the stairs          one flight          from myself          heading away towards myself

everything's identical          door beside door          smoky kitchen stink
               garbage eggshells

selfsurrender          on the stairs spiralling up          round an unseen axis
               on the landing

anyway my clothes          got up in human guise          shit not being able to do
               without that yet

abominable          bringing me to this          I won't go outside          I crash right on in
          with it          pay attention          see this and freeze


*from Svidrigailov's diary*


such a modest killer you          I beg your pardon          in your ruthless virginity

believe you me          sooner or later morals          need protection from virtuousness

there'd be fewer murders          my dear Raskolnikov          many more surprising joys


hands over his face          5000 years' experience          fuckers          and him peeking
               through his finger

just the way          the Let's Make Believe con gets off          rotten trick with greasy
               cards

as though you as though I          as though we all          weren't the products of
               lovemaking

phony you'd love subverting succession          you've no right despising the inception




*Sándor Rákos* / 131

nor can you preach virtue          unless you were conceived in soil          through c
                                              of the familiar ways

you suspect me          you go on repeating it          what's my reply          I suspect you

you protest too much          you're well aware          of what you despise in me

ascetic          the sensualist's alter ego          perverts in reverse          snapping yo
                                              whips over everybody

I could say          I chose fornication          on epistemological grounds

why cheat          myself and the other          I stick to the palpable

you believe eternity's          an idea          you're quite certain

the senses can't comprehend it          vastly huge          vast          and if it's purely opposi

a laundry          think of it like that          utterly sooty utterly cobwebbed

utterly filthy          a tight little junkroom          its corners lost in obscurity

it turns out maybe          it's all there is          you're famous forever and ever

we're passing everything up          merely for that          cockroaches scuttling throu

he meditated at length          while he murdered the crone          and her niece

from the outset I          spat at divine, helpful grace          to be taken for your
                              good citizen your heroic patriot?          not me

from opposing directions          we both crossed the line          made it out into t
                                              endlessness of no man's land

take your pick          Rodion Romanovich          a bullet          or Siberia

for your third option          the voyage          in all its ambiguous strangeness

it could mean escape          adventuring          lots of other things too

but the voyage        let's look at it objectively        doesn't match up to the
                    bloodied axhandle or Porfiry's hypocrisy

my one and only skin's        too precious        to risk for anything

okay        I like this case not one bit        still, I don't care

why shouldn't the strong torture the weak        just leave me out of it


*from Porfiry's diary*

galloping in place        you whip it        Svidrigailov

it whines under you        until it foams        you beat it towards the line

scrotum tightening        jockey with streaming nipples        tough-thighed horseman

I got a whiff of it        it disgusted me        yes        I bet the better mount

privates stuck together        before a greedy mirror


exposing        you're depraved that's what        what clothing conceals

I unwrap the idea        (the soul, so-called)        from its garment of flesh bone
                    word and silence

I reveal the brain like genitalia        I touch I finger it

I force an entry        I conquer        I copulate with it

supreme delight        continuously        orgasm enduring months

two brains in intercourse        coming with an idea        instead of semen


minstrels        caterwauling to the moon at full        outside locked gates

they'll gibber anything        piercing rod        scalpel

breaking it down to its parts        searching its source        love's for a demented surgeon      blindman's buff      anatomy panting away

only those whom logic blinds      pursuers and pursued      dare play it out
the end


Svidrigailov      you keyholing hero      never all at once

sniffing around      vulturine beaked      dropping from ambush

unlike us      a wild game's obsessed ones      possessed ones

a demon will act      blindfolded even while pondering

him too      the proud one      I'm simply hugging to death

noble heart      a grand soul      this starving student

reserved sensitive      chaste      could even be a girl too

a bronco saddled      breaking such a pride      he kicks, bites

I let him buck      froth gushing from him      till he collapses

and calms down      tearing at the halter      Raskolnikov


away from me      dashing in useless rings      running from me thinks he

to me      we're acquainted with this harmless selfdeception      he's run
towards me from way back wh

from fire or to fire      nocturnal beetle      circling the flame

round me      always round me      he can't even breathe without me

murders      like a cashbox in the market-stall      anyone can break into i

how many different needs drive      that one loitering nearby his guilt        if he's got some        isn't the blow of the ax

his downstroke        follows inevitably

he killed the weaker        from weakness        a weak arm

which is why he's trembling        hiding        from me towards me


don't take up arms against arms        the son of the carpenter commanded

even your persecutors        even them shall you love

not many defended so definitively the transgressor who always needs defending

with their Christ's own word we weave not joy for the brows of the weak but a
                    crown of thorns


such a hypocrite you are Svidrigailov        pretending you're indignant

you'd rather not know        lust for power drives you        in your obscene dramas

you want to possess        drool over        put your brand on

so why are you turning aside        like a blushing maiden

when Violence        with its sophisticated tools        is committing rape under
                    your very eyes


Sándor Rákos / 135

GYÖRGY SOMLYÓ: born in 1920, in Balatonboglar, the son of the poet Zoltán Somlyó. He studied at the University of Budapest and the Sorbonne, with an emphasis on French, philosophy, and folklore. He has worked at administrative positions, as a playreader, script editor, magazine editor, director of the Literature Department of Hungarian Radio, and edited *Arion*, a multilingual poetry yearbook published by Corvina Press, Budapest. He has traveled in Eastern and Western Europe, and China. The three volumes of *Hármastükör / Triple Mirror* (1970) were selected writings. Later poems appeared in *A mesék könyve / The Book of Tales* (1974), and a French selection translated by Guillevec was published by Gallimard as *Contrefables* (1974), and in *Épp ez / Just This* (1976). Author of a four-volume collection of essays on poetry and a study on the poem Milan Füst. He has translated French, English, and American poets.

# AND JUNE . . . ?

Complement to a poem by Hölderlin
*April und Mai und Julius sind ferne.*
*Ich bin nichts mehr. Ich lebe nicht mehr gerne.*


April May   July
   (and June?)
And June?
It will be just as old anyway.
(Or hasn't it ever been?)
Has it just dropped from time's rotting fabric?
(Or was it caught by the crazed brain's sieve?)
A once-upon-a-time's
lunar cycle
gone never-never?
A June tabooed,
unmentionable?
A bull that stampeded out of the herd of months?
Or a member broken off marble time?
A year sans June, inimitable?
(Or an inimitable year,
all Junes?)
Time hacked away down to its torso
or fulfilled, period?
An incomprehensible erasure on a page of the past?
Or the illegible hand of a message meant for the future?
That unforgettable forgotten
June
by which April May  (July)
will also forget themselves

A traumatic June
sunk
beneath times lost
submerged in the inconscient
that stole itself out of turning time
An integer lost from the series
making the calculation of the soul all wrong
an extra number
untraceable

György Somlyó / 137

lacuna-June
June with its window smashed
by the stone of its own glory
with its equinoctial balance that cannot be tipped
with its deranging unexpected storms
A June that has never been
and yet cannot end
because it never came to pass
Bull-June
strayed from his herd
careening crazed towards our ranks
wading over into our healthy brains

unmentionable

1977

## TODAY

4 September, 1980

The cat's sitting at the window Darkness
Slowly coming down On the road lights
Slowly lighting up In the unimaginable
Spatial and terrestrial upheaval Among collapsing
Stars Disintegrating societies
Among loves on love's treadmill
In a still more unimaginable
Order and the Scales teetering poised today
Between Nature and man Light
And darkness Darkness
Deepening slowly The lights on the road
Slowly growing brighter The cat's
Sitting at the window It's today Tomorrow
Will be tomorrow

# MARGINALIA

*to Predrag Matvejevic*
*for a literary roundtable*


I
as though our hides were the paper
we read off into the microphone
as though our own hearts were the microphone
that booms inside alone
as though the paper were our hides
that we can't flay


II
even with the ultra-shortwave
simultaneous translator in our ears
we're silent, each in his own language


III
by what sort of generative grammar
would it be possible to untangle the dialogue
from the soliloquy
by what sort of transformation
change dialogues
into our own words again

so that others in us
so that we in others


IV
round world —
 — roundtable
roundtable —
 — round world


V

    *to Chen Huangmei*
    "Ten thousand writers fell victims
    to the Cultural Revolution," said Juen Jung
    the new Secretary of the Chinese Writers
    Union, on the Hungarian Radio.


György Somlyó / 139

the speaker
takes the floor on the hecatomb
of his ten thousand peers
now gone forever
he balances carefully
on the slick ground
as though he himself cannot comprehend how it's possible
that he is not among them
under himself

VI
but are we not
survivors
all who are alive
each a separate ring
of mankind
mutilated millionfold
and still always bringing forth new rings
from its remaining rings
on the ground slick
with its own millionfold mutilated body?

VII
we ringworm Knights of the Grail
outliving ourselves
at the roundtable
is there any kind of Grail anywhere
anything hidden
we might be questing for?

Zagreb, 15 May 1980

# MIMESIS

Ten longstemmed purple tulips
in a clay jug, blackglazed with yellow spots
just to copy
just to trace an outline
just to touch that matter
just the curved stems
just the petalled patterning
just the spaces
just the degree of tilting
just the poised turning dance
of these wild dervishes
of these girls dancing to death
of these gay martyrs
not giddy and vain creation
just mute humility
the one impossible act
just to copy precisely
to make it once more what it is
what it is no more
with mute humility to discover
its ontology and teleology
the pre-flower pre-stem pre-petal
the pre-word word
that will once more unfold
ten longstemmed purple tulips
in a clay jug, blackglazed with yellow spots

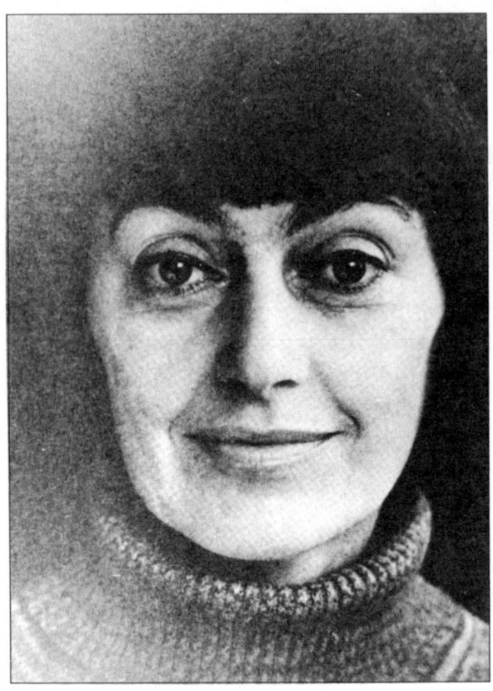

MARGIT SŹECSI: born in 1928, in an industrial slum district of Budapest. After studying at Budapest University, she was on the staff of the literary magazine *Csillag*, then worked as head of a cultural center at Pécs. She was awarded the Attila József Prize for poetry in 1957 and 1968. She has published eleven volumes of poetry, including: *Március / March* (1955); *Angyalok Strandja / Angels' Beach* (1956); *Páva a tüzfalon / Peacock on the Partition* (1958); *Új heraldika / New Heraldry* (collected poems, 1967); *A nagy virágvágógép / The Great Flower-Cutting Machine* (1969); *A madaras mérleg / Scales with Bird* (1972); *A szent buborék / Holy Bubble* (1974); *Birodalom / Empire* (1976); *Kolto a Holdban / The Poet in the Moon* (1984). She is the widow of the poet László Nagy.

# ANGEL WITH HORN

I'm not about to lay off the real Muse,
my own true darling Angel with the Horn.
Not that celestial one so graceful up there,
but curlyhead in the Park at the Fair —
though his robe drapes to his feet, I'd swear
he's been all boy from the hour he was born.

I'm not about to lay off the real Muse:
I hope he'll be the one to bury me instead,
tucking me in with my poems like a shroud.
And, since faithfulness makes them laugh out loud,
I cheat on him first with ideas — a flirt, proud —
lest the shame of the betrayed wreathe my head.

Yet how my body recalls our joined fates:
ah, that sight at the Fun Fair in the Park,
where the tops of the tents twinkle with frost,
and meteors are fodder for the rockinghorse —
ah, that sight: there, beneath the world's hooves lost,
we two, pounded down, cast out into the dark!

A spinning world! And those bearing its burden
are driven off here into this isolation,
those who came round at last from the back door,
who believe that love is worth fighting for,
who have nowhere to love, though old and poor,
all, banished in the snow, an entire nation!

Come, bring me my crown, let the poet rule,
sovereign once more as we used to be.
Before we're thrown, let's dismount its mean back,
let us float above this life that they exact —
you'll do, just you and half my land, this tract,
are quite enough, my angel love, for me.

So come, mister nobody, come on, honey,
fork out your bread, kiss me, and be dutiful.
We were once for real, the fairytale pair,
idyllic lovers death's profaned down there —
those neat landscapes the storm-falcon's despair —
though our four wings are still so beautiful.


## THE HOVERER


You, worldwinged, Hoverer:
trampled in the stony wastes,
wings bent back and crushed,
quivering yet, and dropping into death:

your voice, guided by the song,
your veins, the branching olives —
Long live the first who said, No!
We won't fly for ourselves alone!

Godless the mineral meadows,
our planet's blank plains beseeching —
and we won't fly for ourselves alone,
though we die, and by ourselves alone.

You, dragged down, rejected
by the empty megalopolis of stars
still ruled by The Great Bear,
that inverted, vacant realm

where death comes, an absolute:
falling skyward is better
and you, poised, hovering winged,
tilted now, falling towards Man.

Over these mountains of skulls,
these cities of heads, forests of hands,
glides your shadow, crossing us —
we won't fly for ourselves alone.

Soaring death-bearing for heaven,
flying far as the Star of Love,
knowing your oil must run dry:
how much your wings have cost you!

We trust in heights, and in ourselves,
we long for the dust of the stars.
Arms widened to wings in childhood,
we purred and roared like planes,

and when the packhorse loads
flattened us, could you have believed
your freedom was there in the dirt,
and that earth is the dust of stars?

Sandstorms: and the sandships
are drifting by above you now,
their quartz keels holystoning you
to nameless skeletons. You are free.

You, flying even through the dust,
you, Bird, and Hoverer!
What might have been belongs to you:
these skies thrown down, and crushed.

JÓZSEF TORNAI: born in 1927 in Dunaharaszti, near Budapest, son of a railroad switchman. He attended a business secondary school, but worked afterwards in a truck plant as grinder and later as technician, before devoting himself to writing. He is currently editor of *Kortars / The Contemporary*. He writes criticism, book reviews, essays, does broadcasting work, translates English, American, French poetry and folk poetry from various countries, and contributes regular film criticism to *The New Hungarian Quarterly*. He has published ten volumes of poetry, including: *A bálványok neve / The Names of the Idols*, a selected volume (1970); *Tizenhét ábrándozás / Seventeen Pipedreams* (1976); and *A többszem'lyes / The Many-Eyed One* (1982).

# ARS POETICA

One fine day I'll start writing
     and I'll go on
          night and day
seven days without stopping,
     because finally I have to pump out of myself
Hungarian summers, Europe, the universe:
     those gamboling, black rams on snowy
heights,
the magical black-and-red beetles
     dragging each other through the sand.
     I'll write my arm out in stars,
my legs in blood-boltered ash trees, so that words
     may be transmogrified into all my organs
          one after another
          but then
        I'll pull the pen from my hand,
     and dip it into the river's icy foam,
just as burning, molten
meteors
        are usually snuffed out.


# PSALM

What shall become of us, O Sun,
lacking leg and lacking arm
lacking ear and nose,
lacking eye, lacking mouth
lacking touch and loins, lacking wall, lacking roof,
lacking the gate and lacking the road, lacking god
and lacking death,
lacking tears, and vision?

# SOLAR ECLIPSE

Gone dark now in my insentient time
lashed to myself stretching out
and thinking of my aging long ago foreseen
opening and closing my eyes
hurling myself in memory against
the black, shoreward tide carrying me
back into the roar of even greater blocks of darkness
into the floundering. No green happiness or dusty-hued unhappiness
in this solar eclipse; paralysis, owl's feather soft and smooth,
grub of this futility, I twitch just once or twice,
blind, fetid, disgusted, puking
images over the unseen country up there.
Gone dark now, you ten women,
into whose blood I so often poured,
you ten pines, whose immobility I heard,
tossing myself from darkness to darkness:
petrified in this stone of darkness,
gnawing myself into it, I can't see into myself either,
can't wrap time in its threads,
the whole web glueing to my mouth,
my chest, my soles; swaddled so
and ingrown with hair, heaving myself round myself
yet ignorant of the spasms,
the darkness, the casket's confines, the skull I fractured
forcing myself in; yet dropping
into myself and the primeval ooze,
going dark, it's nothing: we've all witnessed
these things, water dashed upon the embers
banked with coals, blind, broken,
heaped. And I hurling against
the shoreward tide crying but why now,
and for what, yet trembling with the torch
of what words before that even greater darkening?

# TEN THOUSAND NATIONS

Why am I so halfhearted, so doubtful
on these Magyar Plains over which
ten thousand nations hurtled into Europe,
ten thousand retired to Asia,
ten thousand to this salt grass sea of nothing?

why are my eyes so ancient
my feet so halting over the indifferent, eternal prairie
on the way to our squalid home of clay-and-wattles
where my mother's bloodied, joyful thighs
opened for me?


# THE NAMES OF THE IDOLS

These are the names of the idols:
Fate, Invincible King, Gilt Agony,

Your hair's a dimmed theater,
a block of buildings blown up at night,
a derailed coal car,

Your hand on the feverish boy's eyes,
but I see dance steps, tusks,

Your hair's a reed skiff,
tarred harpoon biting my breast,

the almond petal, the carcass carried by water,
a crucified dog in the market,

Your hair's a summery cane shed,
an iron gate opening black,
a Black church,

These are the names of the idols:
Fate, Invincible King, Gilt Agony.

Istváⁿ Vas: born in 1910 in Budapest. He studied at a business academy in Vienna, returned to Budapest in 1929, and worked in various minor clerical jobs before World War II. He has been an editor at a publishing house since 1946, and in that capacity has traveled to most countries in Europe. His publications include: *Mit akar ez az ember?* / *What Does this One Man Want?*, a two-volume edition of collected poems (1970); *Az ismeretlen isten* / *The Unknown God*, collected essays and criticism (1974); *Onarckép a hetvenes évekből* / *Self-Portrait from the Seventies*, poems (1975); *Itt voltam* / *I Was Here*, poems (Szépirodalmi, 1976); *Összegyűjtött munkái* / *Collected Works* (Szépirodalmi, 1978); *Mért vijjoig a saskeselyű* / *Why Does the Vulture Screech?*, memoirs (Szépirodalmi, 1981); *Nehéz szerelem* / *Hard Loving*, autobiography (Szépirodalmi, 1983); *Ráérunk* / *We Still have Time*, poems (Szépirodalmi, 1983); *Megis* / *Nevertheless* (1985).

## ANACREONTIC

Once again seated below bright awnings, here, there,
Pest and Buda. Where'd he turn up from this time,
The half-mug of beer before him? The usual cigarette
in his teeth, dragged at, a drug.
He starts, palms the butt, glancing round,
what's he scared of? The usual raid,
or somebody sees he's alive and turns him in?
No more roundups, no one could hurt him now
with a tip-off. He's still scared though, gets up,
looks round in stifling summer heat as if muffling himself
in his rough scarf, about to get lost in the crowd.
Perky again, you raffish geezer,
because you're on the street for now?

The breakout's making tracks.
Your ID's not been checked out.
He pulls at the smoke and blows it out.
Leans back again under the bright awning.
He's into today alone. Tomorrow's tomorrow.


## A NIGHT WITHOUT LIGHT

She gets up. Her husband never wakes.
Sets off towards him through
the cold night. The other has sneaked out too.
They know which way to turn,
it seems, along the city's hollow-
echoing streets, where, up there
in those big, high, unheatable rooms
thick logs roast
in a fierce, wild fire in the stove,
and dark Persians are spread close by;
they strip, proud of their bodies,

István Vas / 151

the bones, the skin, that striped skin,
green flames breaking free, erupting
from their carnivorous bodies twisting
beside the russet embers. The blowing winter wind, the winter wind
that blows amongst the ruins. Blows through vaster rooms.
The russet, the green flames go out.
Two solitary shadows go off two ways,
in the night without light going their two
different ways, one crossing the new bridge,
the other over the old. Two poor, lonely, carnivorous beasts
returning alone to their dens.


# EQUINOCTIAL


Cold beams chinking
overclouded flashing
great bridges stretching themselves
sludge in the river shining

Gull's cry vanished
eddying northwards
On both shores the gray city
blown by seawinds from the southwest

Archaic bows
are drawn by familiar archers
Tense yourself my nerves
The target's being placed for you

# FORUM ROMANUM

Stones no longer interest me
Neither does history
My eyes find it hard
to make out the Latin
cut in the stones
Nothing interests me anymore
Only whatever I can believe in
when it happens to come my way
I'm going it unsteady and alone
on the road I first took
Where are the Romans now


# HISTORY OF LIT: A COMMUNICATION

Those old letters have turned
into contributions to philology.
Posterity's ignorance perhaps won't comprehend
that battle long ago, that passion.
A woman's leg occurs in some sentence,
almost incidentally, it seems.
I hope it isn't noticed
by the literary historian.
It's the one item that counts for me —
to hell with all the rest!
I saw that leg flare out.

# IDLING

At leisure, idling patiently, lost
as ever in a daydream of the future,
I stand waiting in the summery garden,
as though there were still an ocean
of time rocking quietly before me.

No hurry. No need to write more poems.
The watermark of silence on white paper.
Why smudge it with the pencil?
I must filter some message from that too,
and that message has to be unlocked.

The future's firing-lines flash out
everywhere, and so do destiny's.
Sky, garden turning dark as I stand idling.
The same code both outside and within —
unlocking it my only job.

I'm not sending — the message is sent to me.
Name it, for lack of something better, infinity —
whatever manifests itself silently.
Listening to the silence, I've nothing at all to say.
Shall I at least be granted understanding?

Lines, diagrams invisibly zigzagging
through the darkness, though I can see them
even with my eyes pressed shut.
Coming together imperceptibly,
can they make a picture that makes sense?

O inscapes, you are my true other world!
I am walking along a closed frontier.
The forbidden zone lies beyond, obscured.
Some day I'm going to stumble on
a crossing place that has no guards.

# JUST THIS

Their auburn or black hair, curly hair
or straight, their eyes, dark, brown, gold
or green eyes, their noses, straight, hooked,
long or pert, retroussé, noses, their mouths,
thick, rippling, thin or hardset mouths, their hands,
white, childlike or whittled bones, active hands,
stained by paint, sun, nicotine,
their magical fingers, their breasts, just barely rounded,
small hills or divine, muscular breasts,
their feet, tender and small, or strong, sleek feet,
their shin thews, ankle-power, their yellowed, stamping,
pink, earth-strolling soles, long thighs, the flexing arches
of buttocks we'd have mentioned, had we been brave
enough, though for that matter Attila Jószef discussed
a girl's stomach, the slag revitalized in the gut
tunnels and hot kidney pumps — but one thing
we've never said before, not even its name,
except in execration, the name of our one joy,
and of the shells', the calyxes', of wings, altars,
winged altars, of the incendiary, maddening,
silken vehicle of flavor, spice — this four-letter word
we've never mentioned, never this name
we'll know longest of all.

        A splendid death I'd have,
beyond pain, consciousness, beyond the edges
of the uttered word, if I said no more from
these compressed lips of mine, no more than this,
nothing but this, and only this.

István Vas / 155

# ONCE MORE

You're so brave, you camp-followers of Cain —
after Baudelaire, yet! Shit-shoveling first father,
your visa was validated
when that cretinous cudgel whammed the wandering
flock's shepherd, that day-dreaming pastor,
the smoke of whose sacrifice could rise
up, while yours charred on the ground.
Murder — sanctified as Mutiny
by the flaccid, spunkless nostalgias
of theoretical speculation — remains
what it always was: fingered machine-gun trigger,
the rocket too: that antique club. But instead of expert,
pusillanimous sin, I dare, yes! to praise once more
the pristine challenge of Goodness, its unknown continents,
and the Right-Hand Thief brave enough to be sorry for his sins.


# PORTS

I
That leviathan tanker
tilts on the flank
of the derelict dock
Biggest of Adriatic ports
A rusty tramp homebound
The little ferry coming in fast
A blue boat sailing out's a patch
melded in minutes into the lighter blue
Over my head and over the ships anchoring
a huge canary container
in the talon of a giant crane
floats to the dock as a freighter loaded with fat logs
slides into port

Or as the small bay dimming
The island smoothing out in black
The splash more easily heard the scent
of gillyflowers attacking now
And the yacht sidling next to the jetty
just a pale signal as though
fleeing unremarked nevertheless

the fishing smack dark but with subdued calling coming in
and lulling itself asleep — until tomorrow
Or like that single blue single yellow lamp
topping a mast outside the roads
on the high seas by now — or still
or outward bound? Whence where to or where is it nowhere
Or like the campanile that stands up white
amidst those narrow houses of worn gray dolomite
climbing the hillside and tolls across the bay like

II
Appearing unmoving
big and little ports really only transitory
coming going loading unloading reloading
landing slipping out under whatever
flag whatever ship
You see now it's here now not
So the cargo's what counts but it's taken off
taken on by another vessel or truck or train
The flag crew ship cargo always changing
Only the port the same
Port of transubstantiations

III
So, I'd sail
if I could to that dark island
my back towards that sound
They're looking at me, yet I'm still here
in an instant not here nor there
Only to understand that
one separates from the ego
on water land anywhere
rid of cargo
as the signal light beckons

IV
So if you could
mount an assault
into the darkening
like the gillyflower's scent
Sail out like a ship
unremarked cutting the waves
into blue black seas
to find those vast lands
of the nonself
for human conquest
or admission

V
And not retreat
And knowing no more than that
Letting slowly go what
lets us go

Retreating across proofs
chain of compromises
And if all compromise is at last overthrown
Accepting one even worse
Swift in time for it
and netted in shame
Not asking, What's required
but following the sordid command
About face about face

VI
When it's only forward march that counts
Though we never made up that one
Still, to have it occur to us is something after all
considering the circumstances, I mean
Prow cutting the water is what counts always
And if that sea's not blue-black
but black, wine-dark, or lead-gray —
what's the difference? what is the difference?

Compass, rudder, destination
Lose your cargo and the port's sealed to you
No ship runs in missing its ensign
Irregular papers can be overlooked:
bills of lading, commission, license —
what's the difference? what is the difference?

But, intact your cargo must be, your crew, your flag
What's dumped or used right there
or what's designated for a change unknown
What's transferred to where — all to be decided
when everything is in
The port of transubstantiations


# TAMBOUR


Whence, hardworn drum
winging past death
natural, unnatural
through siege and shelter

wan goatskin face
stained with coal cellar dust
raised again with the sweat
of palms beating out the dance

fingers dancing, and sticks
of glossy wood, bloodclot-brown
flat palm flicking
counterpoint, tapping soft
syncopated commands staccato
on the smooth parchment

Drum, resurrection drum
out of its opened mouth
swarm the lifted knee
taut rounded buttocks
tight legs
leaping burning soles
the hair floating in flight

Sounding box, drumming
its wan death's skin —
victorious, true portrait
its blackened face
making its accusation
with the searching, sceptical hand
the fugue erupting, shaking
its captive soul, the dance


## THE LADDER


What's to be done with that ladder
leaning against the cherry tree? When was it worth
climbing into the top of the tree for cherries?
Where are the cherries now? The grapes are full.
Someone's quick fingers are flipping
the calendar's loosened leaves.
Shut our eyes to it? No, let's open them,
open wide. Let's look, see to the very end!
Though trying not to be dizzied. Because the neglected
garden's wheeling around and around.
The garden's emptied out, the garden is still here.
And there's the ladder, leaning
uselessly against the naked cherry tree.

# THE LION

The power of the celestial Lion is broken,
his blazing ardor decreasing:
after nights of showers of stars
the late-summer sun strolls leisurely
like the old lion in his cage.
It was the female who wanted what might be
love's last encore, not he.
She pressed against the male's flank, her great,
yellow body coyly begging,
until he rose at last stretching slowly
and with some trouble mounted her
as she lay flattened with devotion. The male
was about to roar, but could only
gargle. Finished it fast, with
what strength remained. Then slid off.
Stretched out, panting and exhausted.
The female sat up, refreshed,
and licked his body with gratitude.
He was grateful too. Lifted his maned head
and rested it on her. They smiled.
We were standing there, young lovers,
beyond the bars, a current flashing
through us! Quick! Home! To Bed!
But we just stood there, watching them a long while:
how lovely the love of old beasts of prey!
The flare of cooling bodies.

# THIS TOO IS ARS POETICA

*from conversations of Einstein and Heisenberg*


World, *natura*, phenomenon:
unimaginably complex.

Must be reduced, you understand? brought down
to simpler forms.
The little child says, "Ball. . ." How many
and how many sorts of sense perceptions
and phenomena it condenses in that word!
Or, are we to believe this ball exists —
for a fact?
                    Still, it's true:
nature's laws are simple.
And, strictly considered, this simplicity
has an objective character. Nature itself
leads us to marvellously beautiful,
simple, mathematical
forms.
                    What are you saying, colleague,
do you class form and beauty
amongst the notions of physics?

Yes, Professor. Put it this way —
weren't you ever startled by the elementary,
almost scary, completeness of those
complex connections nature extends
before our eyes?
Well, those suddenly unfolding forms
always surprise us. Furthermore,
I believe form gives birth to law.

Is that so? Then maybe that space-equation
could be even simpler. . .more elegant.
Which won't be easy. I mean,
let's not forget
that hope as well as what's possible tomorrow
is an indispensable
element of human existence.

Endre Vészi: born in 1916. For a while, he worked as a steel engraver, publishing his first poems while a teenager. In addition to being a poet, he is also a novelist, playwright, and scriptwriter for radio and TV, frequently focusing on recent history hor subject matter. The movie of his novel, *Vera Angi / Angi Vera*, won the Grand Prize at Cannes in 1979. He has published ten volumes of poetry, the latest being *Válagatott Versek / Selected Poems* (1983).

# DREAMING OF THE CASTLE

A door opens in the gray wall
Franz Kafka comes through, stooped
offers his hand, saying, So —
he says, I've come to see you
your whole generation, I mean

I mean, he says, all those
called for this strange trial
whose names are down in the files
who have been made to wait for years
in a windowless room

where the why of it's unknown
everyone will get his
where sawdust's strewn
around the tin potty each morning
around the tin potty at night

Blind yellow puddles of electric light
shadow-prosecutors always scurrying
their briefcases stuffed with shavings
bird nests in the executioner's hat
knives honed by glints of moonlight

keeping silent waiting according to regulations
in front of a door that is no door
keeping silent waiting according to regulations
gripping an iron doorknob
in front of a door that is no door

yellow fingers crease the paper
the one who knows the law by heart
says nothing in falsetto
sleeps through the responses
doesn't leave and doesn't return

Restitution and requital —
you can get away but you never go far
a hundred alleys twist back
the labyrinth eats and excretes
the labyrinth eats and excretes

SÁNDOR WEÖRES: born in 1913 in Szombathely, a town in western Hungary. Weöres studied law, geography, and history, but eventually took a doctorate in philosophy and aesthetics at the University of Pécs (1935). He travelled in the Far East in 1937, visited Italy in 1947-48, and travelled to China in 1959. In 1941-50 he worked as a librarian in the cities of Pécs, Székesfehérvár, and Budapest. He has lived in the capital, devoting himself to writing, since 1951. He published his first poems at the age of 14, and his first volume in 1934. His collected works appeared in three volumes in 1975, containing the complete poems, prose poems, narrative, verse plays, nursery rhymes, and also his doctoral dissertation, *A vers születése / The Birth of the Poem*. His huge output as a translator — collected in three volumes — includes works by Shakespeare, Rustaveli, Shevchenko, Mallarmé, folk poetry and countless classical and modern poets from East and West Europe, as well as Africa and the Orient. His travels have taken him to most of Europe, the United Staes, Egypt, India, and China. A selection in English appeared in *Ferenc Juhasz / Selected Poems*, translated by Edwin Morgan (Penguin Modern European Poets, 1970). Other work includes: *Áthallások / Overhearing* (poems, Szépirodalmi, 1976); *Egybegyüjtött írások / Collected Works* (3rd edition, Magvető, 1975); *Egybegyüjtött műfordítások, Collected Translations* (Magvető, 1976); *Harmincöt vers / Thirty-Five Poems* (Magvető, 1978); *Ének a határtalanról / The Song of the Boundless*, poems (Magvető, 1980); and *Posta messziről / Mail from Far Away* (poems, Magvető, 1984).

# A DREAM OF ROAMING

What is this sad legacy,
always clearing out?
Forever on my way,
never to sojourn here or there.
The train hoots,
and I'm off for the station.
I'd run, but I'm lugging someone else's bag,
where have I lost mine?
And the door I'd like to exit from
won't open.
My satchel gets bigger and bigger
swinging, swagging
against my shoulder, belly, bottom.
I'm finally out of the apartment,
but the stairs are gone,
a chasm deep as the sea at my feet.
No matter, here's a forgotten ladder,
I'm descending the depths,
where miniature valley villas
hide in a whirlpool of foliage.
And now there are no more rungs to the ladder,
I drop, levitating on my luggage,
landing abruptly.

But I'm lost in these valley streets,
which way's the station?
I'm hurrying among alien houses,
there's no street, I'm cutting through yards,
and the buildings are so tall,
all black-fronted,
gold-wreathed like headstones.
At last! here's my station!
But in my haste
I forgot to get dressed,
I'm mother-naked,
which is no way to board the train.
But now I realize there's no railroad here,
though there is a bathtub, soap, hot water —
undressed I climb in, stretch out,
and whatever it is I was after I forget.

Sándor Weöres / 167

# A POEM ON THEATER

When the curtain
    rises
on a space that dwarfs
    us,
hundreds of sharp
    eyes
pierce the hollow
    stage.

Phenomena rustle
    about there,
lit up, glowing
    in the night,
flashing with the sheen
    of metal,
and palaces are built
    out of words.

The play is
    irresistible,
and we look at one another
    when we go,
because we see
    that gentle one
who was king
    in the play.

# A STRANGE CITY

When I left the room
I took a crooked corridor,
and knew I could never retrace my steps.
What a strange city this is,
despite its great, flapping flags,
its roar and its glare.
Near to where
the earth meets sky,
and a vast water cuts across,
part river, part unending rain.
Here I've lost myself
like a child put in my care,
the dense drops from sodden flags
drumming that I'm not me anymore,
as I wander the corridors
through all the city's baffling customary ways.


# A VISION

The cat at the end of the world
dozes on a column of shadow,
below her a thousand streams
go round and round forever.

Rivers, the rainbow,
the whole world tiptoes by
glowing like marble,
and drops into the sky.

Wine fumes drift into the city
from the torrent at its edge.
This age is so deafening
I don't even hear your voice.

# AS THOUGH IT HAD NEVER BEEN

I always wake up
from my dreaming.
I can't tell
where it began.

I always wake up
from my wandering.
It stops as though
it had never been.

I always wake up
from my home.
Strangers are there,
people I do not know.

I always wake up
from my life.
It ends as though
it had never been.


# AT SIXTY

Shadows stand
in the street
waiting for me.

But I've gone beyond
their high noon,
walking without myself
in an undetermined night.

As long as daylight's fate
still shines upon my hat,
my shoes throughout the night
are neither swift nor slow:
my feet are not in them.

# CONTRARIES

Only what is, is forever.
Only what is not never is.
Only what is not is forever.
Only what never is, is forever.

What is always changes.
What is not always is the same.
What is not always changes.
What is always is the same.

What moves not is unmoved.
Restless is what rests not.
Even what is unmoved moves.
Even what is restless rests.

Who lives is alive.
What lives no more is dead.
Who lives, lives death.
Who dies no more is dead.

If you can't follow, go with the flow.
If you follow, be still and move on.
If you follow, stop here.
If you can't follow, just let it go.

It's only what is forever.
It's not only what's not forever.
It's not only what's forever.
It's only what's not forever.

# CROSSED WIRES

I

Action shackled
by force of circumstances,
now on fever to hunt,
now tamed to be still,
now spreading like a whirling wheel,
now folded idly in.

II

The fiddle's caught in the stars' sharp jaws,
nightlong its strings are gnawed,
the mountain, and flesh too, its white flash
of rounded shoulders showing against the blouse,
and raw newborns still tinkling like coins
dropped in the well — those motionless shears, shining.

III

Old, desolate rooms
go hobbling across the street,
shorn of their timepieces
and all their children.
The opened window clatters on their heads,
the Garden about their feet lies dead.

IV

I am dandled on the world
by a marvellous dream.

In the spring wind I munch
on grubs for my lunch.

Butterflies all dead
hatching in my blood.

V

Summer's tendrils scrape away,
demigods dreaming it all comes
home again as they doze, like radishes
waiting for rain in their earth.

VI
The minutes stand ankledeep in water,
drenched in the mirror among the branches,
then march away through the woods.
A pointy star's drinking
from their uninhabited pool.

VII
Why not desert
the leaves and the trees,
and grow colder forever
in the wintry night.

The merry peddler's
under earth,
mudded to the marrow
and whooping.

Sow it here now,
and don't sow there
if, behind it all,
you swallow your steps.


# EARTHQUAKE


    When the roof, the sky,
and the melody too broke
      above the seedling,
      an exhausted, shadowy cube
      tumbled down on the world
in a crackle of crushing hail.

    And nothing at all was left
      beneath the mound,
only the echoing laughter of nothing.
      Water and earth
      proved murderous,
and not even hope could be fed.

# A DREAM

In dazzling
utter darkness
a dream takes me
sweetly by the hand.

It finds footing
through the muck,
draws a bridge
over the swamp,
totes a pack
through nowhere.

Nothing in my pockets,
and not even pockets:
it pays my way
with plenty of nothing.


# ETERNAL EVENING

I sit on a sunstruck wall
and ponder the shade.

The cold stream at my feet
grips my ankles.

It grows, turns dark,
gropes at my chest, my forehead.

It spreads over everything,
everywhere — utter decay.

Quiet — not raging or paralyzed —
a friend from time out of mind.

# EPHEMERAL

The wind loses its fingers reaching out.

The star rapping at the window
says it has never lived,
though everything else has instead.

But so many deserts are here
that heaven itself is too poor to fill them!

Even that which never dies
must perish with them one by one.
And everything beyond the mountain next door
where the fish gather at the weir
to gape at the sea.
And all of it in my room.


# EXCERPTS FROM THE MODERN TRAGEDY

I
The mountain stood here once;
now everything's faded
in the bay night's sailors
set out from, having lost
their fishing gear
in knee-deep water.

Oh, I can still recall the mountain!
and the question we no longer
ask
outlined in utter brevity
in the cloudless sky
on the crowns of stars.

Wooden columns stand alone
weeping moss over the stones,
and we know nothing, we just wait
sadly and in vain.

II
Your animals, shepherd,
walk the skies,
watching for the sign,
though it's yours no more.
Today, I too
could sense the South wind
carrying the forest's currents,
because I cannot wait
to be crushed beneath
the unmeaning, mercifully random boots
of the mighty.

III
We had built with confidence,
then destruction came.
But the building blocks were all fake,
hollow.

If you knew who I am
you would not blame me for my poor advice,
because I was asleep when I was being taught,
I was allowed nothing more,
I was blanketed from east to west
and beyond all the compass points
my dreams now penetrate,
and I forgot it all.

IV
There's no longer any answer.
Only the last question, unfolding its wings like a bird
who'll never come again.
Perhaps it's the cry never cried:
"O, behold this beauty, her hair drooping in the mud,
behold what once was pure, her head emptied now,
O, behold truth!" As for the rest: silence,
then the noise again, the grinding wheels,
and the clamor of the monkeys in the trees.

## GAME

(she says)
Not even listening.
My eyes are shut.
You say, There's a harrowing wind.
Not even listening.
You say, Fire's blazing hot.
My eyes are shut.
You say you love me.
Not even listening.
You say, I'm dead.
My eyes are shut.


## BLEAK

A listless morning,
the country's fogged-in,
besieged
by bleakness.

The crow dance
invades the room,
settles on a chair,
crawls into bed.

Night's last shadows
make a stand in one corner,
a straggler dream
resists the world.

Like a penny
in a dark hall,
I've lost my way
in the ruthless fog.

I'm a ghost,
lifeless,
someone else speaks
for me in the mist.

# MUTTERING

At the top of the years I stand,
dizzied, long past the threshold
of age, and glance into the well
of my sixty-seven years. What if I tumble
and shatter all my former days on its stones?
Dying's not in the past, I know —
it's the present splitting my skull,
and my place is down the well of the past.


# IN THE BEGINNING

Spreading our winged arms before the flames, we offered
to the sun the first stone we picked up. While white birds
recoiled towards the frozen quarter of the compass.
They, the bright-feathered ones, flew into the darkness
and cold. We were still grounded, except in dreams.
(The stone, scored with deep grooves, still remembers.)
Above the stones we carved a great canopy to give space
to our vision. The road ran aloft, following the winged,
fleeing birds; we skipped along, only swinging our arms.
And our starry nights slept in the pit of this concave
cradle. We prayed to the sun. We never glimpsed the shadow.
Darkness was simply our bedroom.
(The grooved stone remembers: it stands in one place.
But which way should we remember, backward or forward? The
canopy we carved to keep time points us everywhere when we
gaze at it.)

# NOISE IN DARKNESS

Not the night of shepherds.
Falling rock,
your face flashing in fog.
The procession pushes on,
swirling those who stay here round and round.

If I'd even once peeped in
at what the veil
of this enormous night conceals!
Only the smoke of repentance,
the dust of crumbling,
and beyond, roof-high,
the pyres of the unknown,
and unseen wheels.


# SONNET MANQUÉ

If at forty you met yourself
as you were at twenty,
you'd be jealous — or slap him.

You're no longer
who you were yesterday.
You're not yet
what you'll be tomorrow.

Memories merely deceive:
death is threaded through life.

Because this "I" constantly
dies, I after I,
the half-baked I in me,
the smarter I with me,
the derelict I on me, the I who. . . .

# STRAY DOG

You nip at the dried burrs
sticking to your side:
nobody's dog out tonight
below a black sky.

Suddenly you stop, spin round
and round like your heavenly star,
nibbling at your side
stuck full of dried burrs.


# THE OWL

When I'm sealed
in night and peace,
listening to the owl
on the garden wall,
death's not half
so threatening
as in the madness and turmoil
of day.

The life of the city
drums in the faraway,
reaching my
forest quiet,
a thousand streets
all one constant noise,
ignorant
of this intimate
passing away.

# RAIN

The rain's pounding away
    at the rusty eaves.
Twirling, sliding, bubbling foam —
    well, that's rain.

You too, and I should walk now
    as free as that
on cloud, on air, the meadow
    and the vapor roads.

Move around up there and here below
    like this liquid thing,
flowing into human life on rooftops
    and on shoes.


# MAGNETIC

A long reach the garland has
reaching hand to hand
through all hands
from outset to ending.
We're stepping over the mountain
Take the garland
Hold it on either mountainside
We're skipping on the sea
Take the garland
Hold it on either shore
We're flying in the sky
amid stars

A long reach the garland has
reaching from hand to hand
through all hands
from outset to ending.

# PROLOGUE TO "THE BOATMAN IN THE MOON"

When I was a child in the little village
they held theater in an unused stable.
It was there I first felt my fever rage
as spooks flitted from the wings, palpable.
The clumsy amateurs I watched were local,
and wandering companies played there too.
Nothing since has ever been more noble
or delightful! They touched me through and through.

I wish that I could act like them,
village-folk performing with such passion
they froze in heat, and glowed in the frost.

This play will be a dream of many colors,
and pass beyond both life and death's borders.
Perhaps it's not written, but dreamed at most.


# UP AND DOWN

Deep in clouds, the winds' home,
   little houses stand all in a row,
whips of celestial fire cut through
   and light flares far away.

You can hear grubs in tufts
   of bushes, between bricks,
life's spirit in everything:
   all things that drift away.

# PROVIDENTIAL

On this moss-fringed isle
    I'll build my fort.
On this isle adrift on still air
    I'll knock it silently together.
On this isle fitting my palm
    I'll set up all my empires.
Hot ones, icy ones.
    Daylight and dimming ones.
Here my loping hounds
    Like gillyflowers slanting in the wind,
My chamberlain, the slumbering mushroom,
    And milkweed, my cook.
I cater the wedding party,
    Friends, relations.
I cater for my sons and daughters
    Who never remark how long ago I died.
When they are grown they'll surmise my trick,
    But where am I then?


# THE GATE OF TEETH

I
The Gate of Teeth, which you came through,
is a red marble hall: your mouth;
its white marble columns are your teeth;
and your tongue's the purple carpet that you tread.

II
A different God-face confronts you
at each window of time you look from.
Lean out of the time of sedge and thrushes:
God strokes you.
Lean out of Moses' and Elijah's time:
God bargains.

Lean out of the time of the Cross:
God's face is bloody as Veronica's Veil.
Lean out of your own time:
God is ancient, bent over a book.


III
Head down like Peter on his cross,
man hangs into the sky's blue, his hair floating,
the earth thumping above his soles.
He who sees him
cannot tear his sleepless eyes away.


IV
Lacking sugar, the child eats
chicken droppings and finds them sweet.
It's all one big lump: what a dull star!
It's all a worm: wingless cherub!


V
If you get to Hell, go down all the way:
there's heaven. Everything returns.


VI
Men build an easy street.
The carnivore tramples a track in the forest.
And regard the tree: how depth and height, and each
        point of the compass is tightly strung from it!
In itself a road in all directions!


VII
When you step through the splendor of the last pair of columns,
your hair touches the dome, infinity in and of itself,
and a swirl of rose-petals lays you out,
and all that spreads below you is your wedding bed:
                    the whole world —


Here you can say:
"I don't believe in You, my God!"
And the storm of rose petals smiles:
"But I believe in you — now are you content?"

# THE PLAIN

A muddy-wheeled cart goes lurching
between the poplar trees' wide rows
just where the narrow track
cuts from the main road.

Crops, naked fields, horizon
and sky surround the single horse
and driver in a wide frame,
hiding them in fixity that never alters.

The distant here seems very near
and what's near seems far away:
all sing together as one —
everywhere furrows, lumps of clay —

horse, driver and small cart
rolling the working hours away
through slow centuries,
and buried by the nights and days.


# THULE

The rasping laughter of sunlight,
waves holding me tight,
exhilarated blood of the rooster,
the rainbow resurrected in thunder
X-ing space at random everywhere —
to you I owe my entire store.

All the little worlds of the large world:
the lamps whose lights are suddenly unfurled,
the bench I'm given leave to squat upon,
my fate shot through by flames hurled
from the sling forever whirled
until this life of mine is done.

Is it to death, or beyond, I must go?
Distant Thule, the land that none can know,
beckons me: the boat's launched from the strand,
the clouds sink lower day by day
and seldom open windows on the way —
yet, there I'm expected on that island.


## UPWARDS


Up, and only up, as the Sun
with his unseen retinue's descending,
haunted by all the ghosts of twilight
gathered in the hollow tree, in folds of bark,

towards the mountain's peak at this late hour,
upwards in twilight! But who could measure
the long journey, the roofless and roomless
celestial descent from mountain to mountain?

"You, you," that echoing comes,
"watch out, your youthful strength is gone,
and no Nefertiti waits at the summit,

nor hanging gardens of Semiramis!" Yet
there's foot-lifting magic concealed in the rocks:
on the way down, as well as upwards.

# THE POETS

| | |
|---|---|
| Beney, Zsuzsa | Born 1930, Budapest. |
| Csoóri, Sandor | Born 1930, Zámoly, Western Hungary. |
| Fodor, Andras | Born 1929, Kapósméro. |
| Görgey, Gábor | Born 1929, Budapest. |
| Hajnal, Anna | Born 1907, Gyepüfüzes, Western Hungary. Died 1977. |
| Illyés, Gyula | Born 1902, Rácegrespuszta. Died 1983. |
| Kalász, Márton | Born 1934, Somberek, Western Hungary. |
| Kálnoky, László | Born 1912, Eger. |
| Kassak, Lajos | Born 1887, Ersekújvár, now Czechoslovakia. Died 1967. |
| Kiss, Anna | Born 1939, Lipila. |
| Ladányi, Mihály | Born 1934, Dévaványa. Died 1985. |
| Nagy, László | Born 1925, Felsöiszkas. Died 1978. |
| Oravecz, Imre | Born 1944. |
| Orbán, Ottó | Born 1936, Budapest. |
| Pilinzsky, János | Born 1921, Budapest. Died 1981. |
| Rába, György | Born 1924 |
| Rákos, Sándor | Born 1921, Újfeherto-Kálmánháza. |
| Somlyó, György | Born 1920, Balatonboglar. |
| Szécsi, Margit | Born 1928, Budapest. |
| Tornai, Jószef | Born 1927, Dunaharaszti. |
| Vas, István | Born 1910, Budapest. |
| Veszi, Endre | Born 1916, Budapest. |
| Weöres, Sándor | Born 1913, Szombathely, Western Hungary. |

The coffee house of 17th-century England
was a place of fellowship where
ideas could be freely exchanged.
The turn-of-the-century Parisian cafes
witnessed the birth of cubism and surrealism.
The coffee houses of 1950s America
hosted poetry readings that continue to
influence literature and society.
We hope such a spirit
welcomes our readers in the pages of
Coffee House Press books.